The Story of Pysanka

A Collection of Articles on
Ukrainian Easter Eggs

Ukrainian Scholar Library

THE STORY OF PYSANKA

A Collection of Articles on Ukrainian Easter Eggs

Sumtsov, Horlenko, Nomys and Others

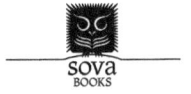

SYDNEY

Copyright © Sova Books Pty Ltd 2019

First published 2019

Editorial Board: Eugen Hlywa (†), Yuliia Vereshchak, Halyna Bondarenko, Serhiy Pjatachenko, Lesia Tolstova, Svitlana Yakovenko

Copy editing: Anita Saunders
Cover illustration: Mariya Luvchieva
Translation: Svitlana Chornomorets

Series: *Ukrainian Scholar Library*
Book 1: *The Story of Pysanka: A Collection of Articles on Ukrainian Easter Eggs*

ISBN: 978-0–9945334–8–7 (Paperback)

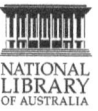

NATIONAL
LIBRARY
OF AUSTRALIA

A catalogue record for this book is available from the National Library of Australia

The folk legends portray the egg as a source of life, and as the universe.

Mykola Sumtsov, 'Ritual egg' (1889)

Contents

Acknowledgements

This publication is a result of the work and support of many people. The backbone behind the *Ukrainian Scholar Library* series for years has been Dr Eugen Hlywa, who passed away in 2017. His legacy for the Ukrainian cultural and scholarly heritage to receive world recognition will live in this series as well as in his own writings.

We are sincerely grateful to everyone, who contributed to this publication. Here are some of the names.

We are indebted to the wonderful staff of the National Art Museum of Ukraine, especially Lesia Tolstova and Yuliya Lytvynets, who selected and supplied copies of the Ukrainian artworks, some of which are included in this book.

We are especially grateful to Tamara Kondratenko and Nataliya Kondratenko from Vasyl Krychevskyi Local History Museum, Poltava, for photographs and other materials in relation to Kateryna Skarzhynska and her museum in Lubny.

Our sincere thanks go to Mykhailo Skop, an artist and Christian iconography expert, for supplying images of Ukrainian Christian icons.

Luba Petrusha deserves a separate mention. For many years Luba has been gathering information about pysanky and sharing it on social media as well as her website www.pysanky.info. Presently her work is one of the most comprehensive sources of information on the subject in English language.

The editorial board did outstanding work on the project, for which we are very grateful.

2019 Foreword

Pavlo Rybalko

Pavlo Rybalko is a senior curator at Kropyvnytskyi Local History Museum. Art of pysanky is one of his areas of expertise. Pavlo Rybalko's publications include a book on Volodymyr Yastrebov's pysanky collection (Rybalko 2010).

This book is a compilation of 19th century articles dedicated to Ukrainian ritual Easter eggs, *pysanky* and *krashanky*. The articles have been previously published in a Ukrainian journal *Kievskaya Starina* [Kyivan Antiquity]. The articles vary in style and length as well as volume and depth of information on the Easter eggs. Some offer a properly structured story on *pysanky* and *krashanky*, their history, characteristics, tales, legends and traditions connected with them, whereas others briefly touch upon the subject and mention the Easter eggs in passing, rather concentrating on other topics such as museums or folk games in Ukraine. The diversity of the writings offers a more comprehensive insight into the significance of the *pysanky* and *krashanky* enjoyed in Ukrainian culture.

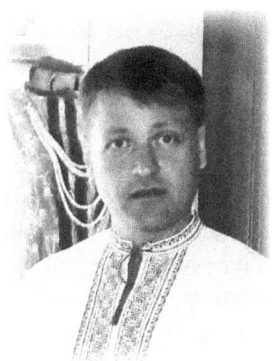

Pavlo Rybalko.

***

The sacred custom to ornate eggs as part of Easter celebrations has been popular among many cultures for centuries. However, it seems that in the Ukrainian culture *pysanka* also enjoys special reverence and is often regarded as a symbol of the country. Thus, in his poem *Kniazhna* (1858), the much beloved Ukrainian classic poet, Taras Shevchenko (1814–1861), turned to *pysanka* to convey the beauty of his native land.

There are monuments and other testaments to *pysanka* throughout Ukraine and abroad. In 1987, the *Pysanka* Museum was established in Kolomyia, Ivano-Frankivsk region. In 2009, the National Bank of Ukraine released commemorative coins 'Ukrainian *pysanka*': nickel silver coins with nominal value of 5 *hryvni* and silver coins with nominal value of 20 *hryvni*. In 2016, 2017, 2018 and 2019 Canada, the country with the largest Ukrainian diaspora, released two silver-coloured coins in a shape and with the design of Ukrainian *pysanka*. Canada was also one of the first countries to erect a monument to *pysanka* in 1974, in Vegreville. Other countries, like Romania and Lithuania, also have monuments dedicated to their traditional Easter eggs. Periodically, some countries of Europe release philatelic and postal products depicting images of their Easter attributes, including eggs.

An impressive assortment of Ukrainian ancient *pysanky* is found in collections of famous world museums, including London, Saint Petersburg, Prague and Krakow. A significant event for *pysanky* lovers took place in 2011, when 210 ancient *pysanky* were returned to Ukraine from Germany, having been appropriated during the Second World War and kept in Höchstädt an der Donau Regional Museum for about seventy years.

For the most part of the last century the *pysanka*-making custom has been suppressed by the Soviet government russification and anti-religious policies. However, during the recent decades various measures have been taking place in Ukraine to offer the original *pysanka*-making art its proper place in the nation's modern culture. The authentic traditions are being revived with the establishment of *pysanka*-making classes, publication of specialised literature, organisation of various competitions and exhibitions as well as enrichment of the museum collections. Thus, in 2012, on the initiative of a modern Ukrainian musician, Oleh Skrypka, and The Initiatives of the Capital Organisation in Kyiv, the first nationwide festival, Dyvo-Pysanka [Wonder-*pysanka*], took place, where 25 giant *pysanky*-models representing styles of each Ukrainian region were presented. Since then, each year, during the Independence Day celebrations these giant *pysanky* are important participants of the event and are carried along Khreshchatyk Street in Kyiv. For the rest of the year, they are kept at various museums throughout Ukraine, awaiting their next parade.

***

The oldest known *pysanky* that have been discovered in Ukraine are ceramic and are dated as far back as the times of Kyivan Rus, approximately 10th–11th centuries (Michajlyszyn 2015, p. 493). As such they became known as 'Kyivan'. Their specimens were found throughout the whole territory of the Dnieper Ukraine. The unique technology of the ceramic glaze decoration of these *pysanky* even today makes us admire the skilfulness of the masters of the glorious Kyivan Rus era.

One of the latest sensational archaeological findings took place in 2013 with the discovery of a goose egg *pysanka* from medieval Lviv (15th–16th centuries).

Throughout the centuries many cultures considered the egg as a symbol of creation of the universe. The world mythologies and beliefs have plenty of examples of the egg being associated with gods of the Sun, Spring and Resurrection; to mention only a few: the Egyptian gods Kneph, Ptah and Isis, the Phrygian god of vegetation, Attis, the Phoenician Adonis, the Hindu Brahma, the Akkadian goddess Ishtar, the Greek gods Helios and Dionysus and the mythical bird Phoenix, the Persian Mitra, the Karelo-Finnish Jumal, the Polynesian Tangaroa, the Slavic gods Dazhboh, Perun, Yarylo and goddess Lada.

The Ukrainian folklore is plentiful on tales that offer their perspective on the view of creation of the world. The most famous among them are tales known to every Ukrainian from their early childhood: *Yaytse-Raytse* and *Old Man, Old Woman and Riaba Hen*. In their sublime simplicity, the tales pass a clue from our ancestors to understanding visible and invisible worlds, nature and universe. The annual rebirth of the New World was encoded in the symbolism of the 'golden egg' in *Old Man, Old Woman and Riaba Hen*, the physical manifestation of which was embodied into ritual *pysanky* and *krashanky* – the allegory of Living, which was born out of the mysterious Nebuttia [Non-being].

With the introduction of Christianity in Kyivan Rus, the ritual eggs as well as some other Pagan attributes were able to survive eradication and were incorporated in the main religion of the nation. In the case of the ritual eggs, they became an attribute of one of the greatest religious holidays, Easter. New legends were born. However, the ornate egg managed to preserve its archaic traits such as symbols inscribed as part of its ornament.

In Ukraine, *pysanka* that was gifted on the occasion of Easter was kept by the gift-receivers as an amulet and protected the household and family from the evil spirits and other misfortunes, such as fire, illnesses and lack of harvest. Also *pysanky* were used in a number of folk customs and rituals, which included beauty spells, tokens of love and commemoration of dead, Easter folk games and home decor (*pysanky* were used to make 'doves' as a room decoration).

The *pysanka* has absorbed the magnitude of Ukraine's beauty, its diversity and colourfulness. For that reason there is such a wide array of *pysanka* designs, names, kinds, techniques and colour schemes. Taking into account *pysanky's* aesthetic appeal, long history of its existence, versatile use in folk customs and meaningful symbolism behind their ornaments it is understandable why so many Ukrainian ethnographers were drawn to the study of this sample of the Ukrainian folk art. Below are concise biographical pieces on some of the ethnographers who either authored or whose names are referred to in the articles presented in this compilation.

***

The present publication is the commendable undertaking to reintroduce valuable 19th century ethnographic materials. Furthermore, now when the articles are translated into English, the English-speaking readers have another resource to learn more about the Ukrainian national mystical treasure, *pysanka*. Despite the seemingly narrow subject, the articles in this compilation disclose broader information that runs parallel to the topic of the role of *pysanky* in Ukrainian culture, and includes everyday life of an average Ukrainian villager of 19th century (see page 127), the state of the printing business in Ukraine (see page 121), folk legends (see page 133) and so on.

This book is a worthy response to Mykola Sumtsov's appeal contained in his article 'Pysanky' (see page 101) to protect and preserve *pysanka*-making art, which in turn would ensure that the authentic role and meaning of the traditional Easter eggs are known to next generations. It seems that this is precisely what this book is aimed at – to keep knowledge of *pysanka* alive.

Mykola Sumtsov

The author of the most comprehensive article on the Ukrainian Easter eggs in the present compilation is Mykola Fedorovych Sumtsov (1854–1922) (Sumtsov 1891). In fact, this book contains two articles written by this author, 'Ritual egg' (Sumtsov 1889) and 'Pysanky' (Sumtsov 1891). The name of Mykola Sumtsov is known in the fields of ethnography and history as an unsurpassed expert on Sloboda Ukraine. In his writings he offered a thorough account of numerous aspects of the Ukrainian folk traditional life and culture of the area, including mythology (Sumtsov 1893), folk songs (Sumtsov 1886) and wedding customs (Sumtsov 1885).

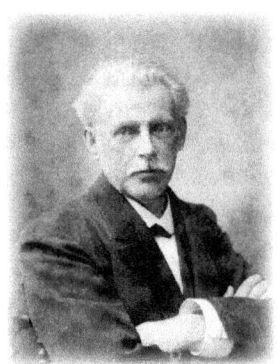

Mykola Sumtsov.

Mykola Sumtsov was born into a well-to-do family, descendants of kozaks. His father, Fedir Sumtsov, originally from Kharkiv, worked in the Ministry of Finance in Saint Petersburg, where Mykola was born. After his father's retirement in 1856, the Sumtsovs returned to Sloboda Ukraine, their homeland.

The leading topics of Mykola Sumtsov's areas of interest included history, ethnography and folklore of Ukraine, which were often presented in a form of a comparative analysis. His fascination with the homeland's heritage was firstly nurtured by his mother, Anna Ivanivna, who brought up Mykola on her own since he was two years old, when her husband died. Later, in his student years, Mykola Sumtsov's choice of studies was supported by his mentor, a philosopher and linguist, a known Ukrainophile, Oleksandr Potebnia (1835–1891) (Mandebura 2011, p. 17). Other outstanding Ukrainian scholars whose works influenced Mykola Sumtsov include Izmail Sreznevskyi (1812–1880), Mykhailo Maksymovych (1804–

1873), Osyp Bodianskyi (1808–1877), Oleksandr Kotliarevskyi (1837–1881) and Mykola Kostomarov (1817–1885) (Dmytrenko 2004, p. 5).

Mykola Sumtsov graduated History and Philology Studies at Kharkiv University in 1875, where he was awarded a gold medal for one of his theses. In 1876 he undertook several courses at Heidelberg University. In 1878 Mykola Sumtsov became a lecturer at Kharkiv University. In 1881 he obtained his Master's degree. In 1885 he was awarded a doctorate and in 1888 he became a professor.

To name only a few topics covered by Mykola Sumtsov in his writings: *koliadky* and *shchedrivky* (Sumtsov 1886), a legend about a sinful mother (Sumtsov 1893), the influence of the Ukrainian scholastic literature of the 17th century on the Russian schismatic literature of the 18th century (Sumtsov 1895), literary tendencies of the Ukrainian writers of the 17th century (Sumtsov 1906) and so on.

During the period of 1889–1890, *Kievskaya Starina* [Kyivan Antiquity] published Mykola Sumtsov's extensive ethnographic observations entitled 'Kulturnye perezhyvaniya' [Cultural experiences], with its forty-first chapter dedicated to the ritual egg (Sumtsov 1889) (published here under the same title, 'Ritual egg', see page 107). This piece is a succinct comparative account of the significance of *krashanky* and *pysanky* in the Ukrainians' celebration of Easter. The author here touched upon the pre-Christian tradition of honouring the dyed egg as a symbol of the Sun and upon the difference of various methods of making the Easter eggs.

Two years later the same *Kievskaya Starina* [Kyivan Antiquity] published another article by Mykola Sumtsov on the Ukrainian Easter eggs, entitled 'Pysanky' (see page 33) (Sumtsov 1891). 'Pysanky' was the outcome of the analysis of a large volume of material based on the author's own observations and information he gathered from others.

The scholar examined publications on the Easter eggs, *pysanka*-making methods and techniques, the origin of various *pysanky's* ornaments and names, the symbolism of the egg in different cultures and belief systems. He also pointed out characteristics of the Ukrainian *pysanky* that were common with other peoples' ritual eggs or which were typical only to the Ukrainian ones. Discussing the aesthetic significance of *pysanka*-making art, Mykola Sumtsov expressed his concern regarding the disappearance of this distinguished form of folk art (Sumtsov 1891) (see page 101).

Mykola Sumtsov was one of the organisers of a regional ethnographic exhibition that was presented at the 12th Archaeological

Congress in Kharkiv in 1902. The exhibits were later held at the Ethnographic Museum of the History and Philology Society at Kharkiv University, which was established in 1904. Headed by Mykola Sumtsov, the museum represented almost all the aspects of Sloboda Ukraine's traditional and everyday life. Interestingly, Mykola Sumtsov also gifted the museum his personal collection of *pysanky*, which comprised of about 380 specimens. The museum was an important scientific and educational institution that greatly contributed to the development of the regional ethnological studies (Mandebura 2011, p. 21). With time the collections of the Ethnographic Museum became the basis of the Hryhoriy Skovoroda Museum of Sloboda Ukraine, which was established following the initiative of Mykola Sumtsov in 1920, two years before the scholar passed away.

Mykola Sumtsov was involved in the work of a number of scientific, educational and public organisations and institutions. He was a member of Poltava and Chernihiv Archive Commissions, co-founder of Kharkiv Public Library, Head of the History and Philology Society at Kharkiv University and many others. His consistent civil and political position, his love for all things Ukrainian – language, culture, literature and traditions, as well as his patriotism – did not quite fit within the Soviet russification policies. As a result, during the seventy years of the Soviet era an unofficial taboo was imposed on the name of Professor Sumtsov. His works were stored in special archive funds and were unavailable for republishing. One could not refer to them in their works in any other way but criticism (Mandebura 2011, p. 7).

After Ukraine gained its independence in 1991, the rise of due interest to Mykola Sumtsov's works and high regard to his persona was undeniable. In 2015 Kharkiv Historical Museum added the name of its founder to its name. The museum also hosts public readings of Sumtsov's works. A memorial plaque to commemorate Mykola Sumtsov was installed on the former Kharkiv History and Philology Society Archives building. These days, the scholars who write their doctoral theses, books and articles on the culture and history of Ukraine have an opportunity to use Mykola Sumtsov's abundant publications as references in their ethnographic researches.

Fedir Vovk

Fedir Vovk (1847–1918, also known as Volkov and O. Kondratovych) was one of the first scholars to conduct extensive research on *pysanka*. At the 3rd Archaeological Congress in Kyiv, in 1874, which was a true apotheosis of the Ukrainian scholars' work of that time, in his speech on the Ukrainian ornament, Fedir Vovk singled out a unique form of folk art – *pysanka*-making. Four years later, he published his paper presenting *pysanky's* leading ornamental characteristics (Volkov 1878). Namely, this work is mentioned by Mykola Sumtsov in his article 'Pysanky' (see page 34).

Fedir Vovk was born in Poltava region, into an old *kozak* family. He obtained his higher education at the universities of Odesa and Kyiv. Being initially interested in natural sciences, he later changed his focus to ethnography and the history of Ukraine. His choice was supported by such prominent Kyiv scholars as Mykhailo Drahomanov (1841–1895) and Volodymyr Antonovych (1834–1908) (Ivanchenko 1995, p. 3).

Fedir Vovk's activities included the establishment of Sunday schools, gathering ethnographic materials and publishing literature in Ukrainian. As one of the 17 founders and a full member of the South-Western Division of the Russian Imperial Geographical Society, he made a great contribution to the Society's work, and, among other things, drafted the division's programme on the subject of collecting ethnographic materials.

Notwithstanding the level of success and recognition Fedir Vovk obtained in his field, he had no choice but to flee his home country due to the threat of arrest since the Russian imperialistic government yet again was toughening its anti-Ukrainian policies. In 1879, he fled to Western Europe, travelling through Bulgaria, where he studied lifestyle and history of the local Ukrainian community. His research resulted in several publications, including an article about the Transdanube Sich (Kondratovych 1883), which came out under the author's pseudonym, O. Kondratovych.

Travelling across Europe, Fedir Vovk explored the ethnographic collections of its best museums, including museums in Vienna, Rome, Bern, Geneva and Paris. In 1887 the scholar settled in Paris, where he wrote extensively, including on the subject of comparative ethnography. In 1905 he successfully defended his doctoral dissertation.

After almost 25 years in exile, in 1903 Fedir Vovk was able to visit Lviv. He was invited by Mykhailo Hrushevskyi (1866–1934), on behalf of the Shevchenko Scientific Society. In 1908 Fedir Vovk made a sensational discovery of the late Palaeolithic settlement near Mizyn village, Chernihiv region, Ukraine. Elements and style of geometrical ornamentation on the found artefacts, which echo in the later *pysanky* ornaments, were thoroughly described by Fedir Vovk's student Levko Chykalenko in his doctorate dissertation (Chykalenko 1923).

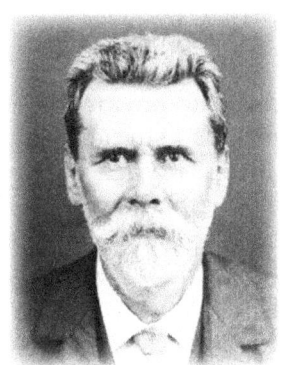

Fedir Vovk.

After the fall of the Russian Empire in 1917, the government of the Ukrainian People's Republic made an appeal to Ukrainian scientists, artists and other intellectuals who previously were forced to leave their homeland to return. Fedir Vovk was offered professorship at Kyiv University. At last, the academic's dream eventuated and Fedir Vovk had an opportunity to return home. However, during his trip to Ukraine, under suspicious circumstances, Fedir Vovk fell ill. He died not reaching Ukraine, in Belarus, where he was buried.

For decades the Soviet government silenced the name of this devoted scholar. His work was labelled as a manifestation of 'bourgeois nationalism' (Ivanchenko 1995), and if ever mentioned, his surname has been translated into Russian, namely 'Volkov'. Fortunately, many of Fedir Vovk's valuable writings survived and now offer rich material for further studies on ancient Ukrainian life and culture, including the art of *pysanky*.

Olha Kosach

A well-known Ukrainian female scholar, whose research pursuits included studies on *pysanka*, was Olha Kosach (1849–1930, also known as Olha Kosacheva, Drahomanova and Olena Pchilka). In addition to her ethnographic work, Olha Kosach was also a translator and writer. She was a younger sister of a well-known political theorist and historian, Mykhailo Drahomanov (1842–1895) and mother of much-loved Ukrainian poetess, Lesia Ukrainka (1871–1913, also known as Larysa Kosach-Kvitka), one of Olha Kosach's six children.

Like Fedir Vovk, Olha Kosach was born in Poltava region. Her parents, Petro and Elisaveta Drahomanovy, who were well-off intellectuals, made sure their children received a good education. It was also Olha's parents who first aroused her interest in Ukrainian folk art and culture. As part of her ethnographic activities, Olha Kosach recorded Ukrainian folk songs and collected samples of embroidery patterns. Also, in 1903, *Kievskaya Starina* [Kyivan Antiquity] published Olha Kosach's extensive research on *koliadky* (Pchilka 1903). She also handed a part of her song collection to a person who probably was the best choice to properly appreciate it, Mykola Lysenko (1842–1912) (Tytarenko 2009, p. 110), a renowned Ukrainian composer. Olha Kosach met Mykola Lysenko when she joined Stara Hromada [Old Community] (1859–1876), a cultural and educational organisation that served as a hub for some of the brightest Ukrainian scholars and artists of that time. The organisation was ultimately banned by the *Ems Ukaz* (1876). There, during the meetings of Stara Hromada [Old Community], Olha Kosach also made acquaintance with Mykhailo Starytskyi (1840–1904), who then became her mentor in the field of literary writing and translation (Vyshnevska 1988, p. 6).

Many years of Olha Kosach's collecting and researching Ukrainian traditional ornament resulted in a publication of *Ukrainskiy Narodnyi Ornament* [Ukrainian Folk Ornament] (Kosach 1876). On several occasions Mykola Sumtsov uses this book as a reference in his article 'Pysanky' (see page 33). The first edition of the book includes an in-depth foreword on the scientific significance of the collected material as well as 31 illustrated pages, 30 of which depict samples of Ukrainian traditional embroidery, and the last, 31st, page depicts patterns of 23 Volyn *pysanky* (see page 50). Olha Kosach's book gained recognition both in Ukraine and abroad. Thus, Alfred Nicolas Rambaud and Louis Léger used it as a reference in their lectures at the Académie des Beaux-

Arts (Tytarenko 2009).

The subsequent revised editions of *Ukrainskiy Narodnyi Ornament* [Ukrainian Folk Ornament] (Kosach 1876) were published in 1879, 1900, 1902, 1912 and 1927. The 1900 edition was presented at the Exposition Universelle, an international fair held in Paris the same year. The edition of 1902 was intended for the 12th Archaeological Congress in Kharkiv. There were also posthumous editions of the book in 1947, 2007 and 2009.

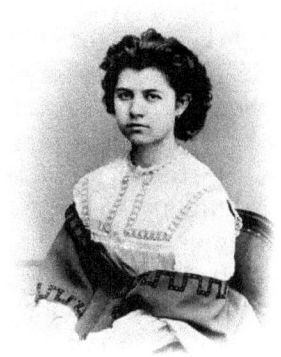

Olha Kosach.

Olha Kosach dedicated much time and effort to her two passions: the women's movement and preservation of Ukrainian identity through its cultural values, including language in the midst of Russian oppression. One of Olha Kosach's achievements in the former area of her activities was the publication of *Pershyi Vinok* [First wreath] almanac (Kobrynska & Pchilka 1887), which consisted of literary works of female authors. Olha Kosach did much to propagate broader freedom for the Ukrainian language, including its re-introduction into the school curriculum. She also organised the supply of Ukrainian books to libraries.

In 1925 Olha Kosach was elected a Corresponding Member of the All-Ukrainian Academy of Sciences (presently, the National Academy of Sciences of Ukraine), where she chaired a number of commissions, including on Literature, History and Ethnography.

Olha Kosach's last published ethnographic researches include articles on the symbolism of roadside crosses in Mohyliv county, Podillia (Pchilka 1925) and Ukrainian traditional village wall ornamentation (Pchilka 1929).

Sadly, the final days of Olha Kosach's life were marred by the attempts of the Soviet

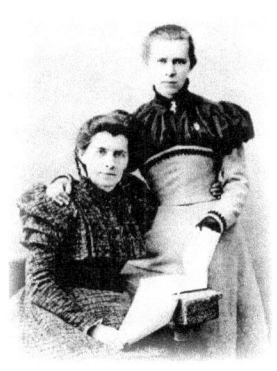

Olha Kosach with her daughter, Lesia Ukrainka.

authorities to arrest her, the 81-year-old paralysed woman. That would have been the second arrest, with the first one taking place in 1920. Thus, the severe illness saved her from the harsh terrains of the Soviet Siberia (the fate of so many of her friends and colleagues) and allowed for her to be buried next to her husband and two eldest children in Kyiv.

The memory of this resolute woman lives in the names of institutions, streets and organisations, both at home and overseas: as for example, the branch of the Ukrainian Women's Association in Sydney, Australia is named in her honour, Olena Pchilka.

One of the most fitting payments of respect to the memory of Olha Kosach was the nationwide Ukrainian project 'The Ethnic Embroidery: Ukrainian Folk Ornament', organised by a known Ukrainian embroiderer, Tetiana Serebriakova, in 2013. Within the framework of this event, in the spring of 2017 a young *pysanka* artist and author Iryna Mykhalevych recreated the 23 of Kosach's *pysanky* (Kosach 1876) and named them 'The Sun Collection' (Mykhalevych 2019). The exceptionally executed *pysanky* were made with only three natural dyes, which created the required seven colours. The artist gifted her *pysanky* to Volyn Local History Museum.

Volodymyr Yastrebov

Volodymyr Yastrebov (1855–1898), a historian, ethnographer and educator, is the author of 'A few words on pysanky' (see page 115), which was originally published in *Kievskaya Starina* [Kyivan Antiquity] in 1895 (Yastrebov 1895). His name is also mentioned in Mykola Sumtsov's article with reference to Volodymyr Yastrebov's research on the use of and customs related to Easter eggs in Old Serbia (see page 64).

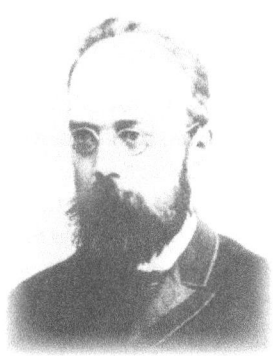

Volodymyr Yastrebov.

Volodymyr Yastrebov was born in Russia, into a family of an impoverished priest. At a very young age he lost his mother and was cared for by his nursemaid, a village girl. He graduated Samara gymnasium and decided to continue his studies at Odesa University. His gymnasium teachers supported his choice, well aware that at the time, Victor Hryhorovych, a renowned expert in the Slavic studies, who was also professor of three universities, was lecturing there (Ch. 1899). At Odesa University Volodymyr Yastrebov elected History Studies. There is an interesting fact from this period of his life. The young man's financial situation threatened his further study at the University. To help him out, his nursemaid sold her sewing machine thus enabling Volodymyr Yastrebov to have means to continue his studies (Braker 2005, p. 6). Under Professor Hryhorovych's guidance, Volodymyr Yastrebov developed a certain approach to history studies, such as allowing for a due consideration of ethnological aspect, for example, the influence of ethnic minorities on the culture of the indigenous population (Bosyi & Bosa 2005, p. 106).

After his graduation, Volodymyr Yastrebov moved to Elysavethrad (presently Kropyvnytskyi), back then a provincial town in the central part of Ukraine, to pursue his career as a history teacher at a People's Education School (Bosyi & Bosa 2005, p. 106), a community type of educational institution, which was not a subject to the Russian imperialistic educational administration. There, Volodymyr Yastrebov was able to dedicate himself to his favourite subject, history, as well as to his pupils. A few years later, when the school administration was passed to the Russian government, the teachers' freedom in their methods of teaching became censored. This event became one of the reasons why Volodymyr Yastrebov left teaching (Ch. 1899). He later worked as the curator of the town's History and Geography Museum (presently, Kropyvnytskyi Local History Museum). With much diligence in three years of his position there, he managed to increase the museum's collection from 342 to 612 exhibits (Braker 2005, p. 13). He also was able to dedicate more time to his research and academic writing on such subjects as ethnography.

During 1878–1897 Volodymyr Yastrebov published a number of historical, archaeological and ethnographic works. His ethnographic works cover diverse topics and include surnames of Kherson county residents (Yastrebov 1893), superstitions, customs and folklore (Yastrebov 1894) as well as traditional and ritual food, such as *korovai* (Yastrebov 1897). He often published his works using a pseudonym or omitting any personal information entirely, fearing accusations of being a free thinker.

One of the leading features of Volodymyr Yastrebov's many works that differentiated them from the writings of his peers was a focus on ethnic minorities that lived in Ukraine and a comparative analysis of their culture with the native population's one. This characteristic is evident in probably the most significant work on ethnography, which Volodymyr Yastrebov was able to complete before his untimely death, *Materialy po Etnografii Novorossiyskogo Kraya* [Materials on the ethnography of the Novorossiysk governorate] (Yastrebov 1894). The publication recounted the pysanka-making techniques and traditions, presented their local names, and described rituals and games that involved the Easter eggs. It also highlighted Bulgarian pysanky, one of which can still be found in Poltava Local History Museum.

Volodymyr Yastrebov began his *pysanky* collection in response to Mykola Sumtsov's appeal published in 1889 (see page 35). Five years later Yastrebov's collection contained 435 *pysanka* specimens. In 1895 *Kievskaya Starina* [Kyivan Antiquity] published his article 'Neskolko slov o pisankakh' [A few words on *pysanky*], which is included in this publication (see page 115), where in addition to Ukrainian and Bulgarian traditional Easter eggs the author mentions Moldavian ones (Yastrebov

1895). The same year Volodymyr Yastrebov donated 59 *pysanky* and 70 watercolour drawings of 65 *pysanky* to Lubny Museum of Kateryna Skarzhynska (see page 111 and page 121). Publication of Serhiy Kulzhynskyi's book *Opisanie Kollektsii Narodnykh Pisanok* [Description of the Folk Pysanky Collection] (Kulzhynskyi 1899) gave an opportunity to many connoisseurs of the Ukrainian folk art to get acquainted with images of Volodymyr Yastrebov's *pysanky*, since it included 121 of them.

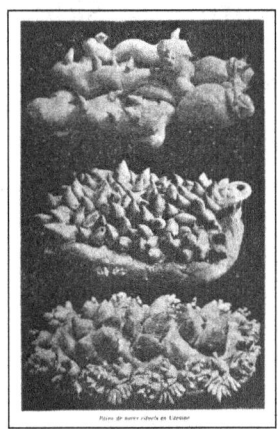

A photograph of ritual breads from Volodymyr Yastrebov's article (Yastrebov 1895, p. 457).

In the penultimate year of his life, when the first signs of a serious illness were increasingly manifesting themselves, *Kievskaya Starina* [Kyivan Antiquity] published his latest works, including *Svadebnye Obriadnye Khleby in Malorosii* [Ritual wedding breads in Ukraine] (Yastrebov 1897). Volodymyr Yastrebov died at the age of 43, in Kherson Zemstvo Psychiatric Hospital and was buried in Kherson where, unfortunately, his grave did not survive. In memory of the scholar, in 1994, Kropyvnytskyi Regional Council introduced the Yastrebov Prize in Regional History, awarded annually on the International Museum Day to selected authors of significant works on the history of the region.

Kateryna Skarzhynska

No research on the role of *pysanky* in Ukrainian culture would be complete without mentioning a prominent woman of the 19th century Ukraine, a scholar, landowner and philanthropist from Poltava region, Kateryna Skarzhynska (1854–1932). Her name is mentioned in this edition several times. One of the articles is dedicated to a museum, which Kateryna Skarzhynska established in Lubny town, and which held an impressive collection of *pysanky*, among its other exhibits (see page 111). Another article is a review of a book (Kulzhynskyi 1899) on the same pysanky collection (see page 121).

Kateryna nee Raizer was born in Lubny town. She received her initial education at home. On many occasions her parents received visits from Kostiantyn Feofilaktov (1818–1901), a geologist and chancellor of Kyiv University (1880–1881), who became one of Kateryna's mentors. For some years Kateryna lived in Russia. Here is one interesting fact from that period of Kateryna's life that launched a whole array of the philanthropic deeds, for which Kateryna Skarzhynska was so well known. At the village, where Kateryna stayed with her family, she established a public school for the local children. At that time, she was only fourteen years old (Serhienko 2015, p. 152).

Kateryna married Mykola Skarzhynskyi, a major general of the cavalry reserve and descendant of an old Ukrainian family. Due to his service commitments the young family had to move from place to place and hence Kateryna Skarzhynska was not able to graduate the Bestuzhev Courses, a women's higher education institution in Saint Petersburg. In 1879 Kateryna Skarzhynska returned to her native Kruhlyk khutir, near Lubny town. There she continued her charitable activities and embarked on a challenging task of establishing a museum. The fact was that Kateryna Skarzhynska gained her interests in archaeology, ethnography and history when she was very young. At the age of nineteen, with the assistance of her nephew, and an archaeologist-enthusiast, Hryhoriy Kyryakov (1805–1883), who was 49 years older than her, she gathered a chaotic but an impressive collection of archaeological findings. Later, thanks to the mentoring of a Ukrainian archaeologist, Fedir Kaminskyi (1845–1891), who was also a librarian and a teacher at the Lubny Gymnasium, along with archaeological excavations, Kateryna Skarzhynska became involved in collecting of artefacts covering all the historical periods, including the rich history Kyivan Rus and glorious times of Ukrainian kozaks.

This collection meant a lot to Kateryna Skarzhynska. She financed some of the local archaeological digs, purchased numerous artefacts, organised a campaign of *pysanky* collections, and approached her neighbours, villagers and friends with a request to send the items, which could enrich the collection. Kateryna Skarzhynska visited museums, such as the Archaeological Museum of Kyiv University, to learn about museum management. In addition to acquiring artefacts, the philanthropist also purchased museum equipment, organised several archaeological exhibitions and, finally, funded construction of a museum building on her estate (Serhienko 2015, p. 153).

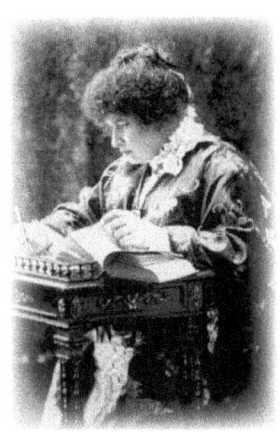

Kateryna Skarzhynska.

In 1885 the museum opened its doors to its first visitors. It consisted of six departments: archaeological (archaeological finds), ethnographic (clothes and pysanky), historical (the early printed books, church artefacts and weapons), numismatic (coins and medals), art (paintings) and natural sciences (paleontological artefacts). Kateryna Skarzhynska ensured the museum had its constitution, which incorporated the main goals of the museum, including its academic and educational purposes as well as free admission for all (Ilchenko 2015, p. 105).

Kateryna Skarzhynska's museum was of interest to scholars in many fields, including historiographer artist and graphic designer Heorhiy Narbut (1886–1920), historian Dmytro Bahaliy (1857–1932), archaeologist Mykola Beliashivskyi (1867–1926) and others. A brief description of the museum's collection, which subsequently became the first private Local History Museum in Ukraine open to general public, was published by Ukrainian writer and folklorist Vasyl Horlenko (1853–1907) in 1890 in

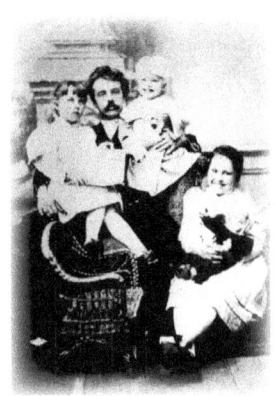

Serhiy Kulzhynskyi with his pupils, Kateryna Skarzhynska's children.

the journal *Kievskaya Starina* [Kyivan Antiquity] entitled 'Skarzhynska's museum in Lubny' (see page 111) (Horlenko 1890).

One of the curators of the museum was Serhiy Kulzhynskyi (1867–1943), an ethnographer and the Skarzhynski's family teacher. It was he who compiled a catalogue of the images of the museum's *pysanky* collection, which totalled 2,219 exhibits. Subsequently, the catalogue was published under the title *Opisanie Kollektsii Narodnykh Pisanok* [Description of the Folk Pysanky Collection] (Kulzhynskyi 1899). A review, or rather preview, of this book is included here (see page 121). One of the original copies of the publication, signed by Kateryna Skarzhynska, is currently located at Poltava Local History Museum.

For her achievements, Kateryna Skarzhynska was offered membership in Moscow Numismatic Society, the All-Russian Society of Natural Science, Anthropology and Ethnography and an honorary membership of Poltava Academic Archival Commission.

In 1906, due to the political situation in the country, Kateryna Skarzhynska donated her museum collection to Poltava and fled to Switzerland. Overseas Kateryna Skarzhynska did not abandon her philanthropy, supporting her compatriots, including socialist revolutionaries. Hence, on her return home, she was not executed as thousands of other members of upper classes but instead was allocated a small pension following Lenin's personal orders. However, a few years later, the Soviet government's attitude towards the woman of the aristocratic background changed and they cancelled her pension. The great philanthropist spent the last years of her life in poverty, supported only by Serhiy Kulzhynskyi. Kateryna Skarzhynska died in 1932 in her beloved Kruhlyk khutir (Serhienko 2015, p. 153).

During the decades of the Soviets' rule in Ukraine, the name of Kateryna Skarzhynska was barely ever mentioned. It was returned from oblivion only after Ukraine gained its independence in 1991. One of the streets in Lubny town and one in Poltava city were named in her honour. The largest part of her museum collection became the foundation of the present day Poltava Local History Museum. A few other exhibits which survived are kept in different district museums and archives of Poltava region. Some of Kateryna Skarzhynska's *pysanky* were also preserved and now are permanently exhibited in the Poltava's Local History Museum. Serhiy Kulzhynskyi's book became a leading source on *pysanky* ornamentation for contemporary artists and ethnographers.

Matviy Nomys

One of the briefest articles in this book was written by Matviy Nomys (1823–1900). It mentions another traditional Ukrainian Easter egg, *krashanka*, and its role in folk games (Nomys 1898). Matviy Nomys is a pseudonym of Matviy Symonov. The name 'Matviy Nomys' is best known to researchers of the Ukrainian folk literature, namely paremiology, as an editor of a colossal collection (about 15,000 entries) of Ukrainian folk proverbs, sayings and riddles, *Ukrainski Prykazky, Pryslivya i take inshe* [Ukrainian Proverbs, Sayings and the Like] (Nomys 1864).

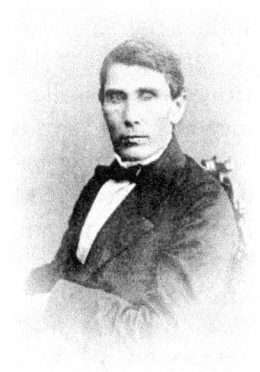

Matviy Nomys.

Matviy Symonov (Nomys) was born into an old well-to-do Ukrainian family. Up until the beginning of the 19th century the family's surname was 'Symon'. In the 1830s it was russified by adding the ending 'ov' to it (Paziak 1993, p. 8). However, when Matviy started publishing his works, he used his original surname Symon to create his pseudonym, by writing the word backwards, 'nomys' (Odarchenko 1985, p. 11). The family's estate was located at Zarih khutir in Poltava region. Matviy's ancestors included kozaks, with one reaching the rank of otaman in Orzhytsia town. Initially Matviy was schooled at home. Then he attended Lubny local school in 1832–1835, Pereyaslav theological college in 1835–1840, and Poltava gymnasium in 1840–1844. In 1844 Matviy Nomys entered the Philological Faculty at Kyiv University, where he graduated in 1848.

Matviy Nomys was not a professional ethnographer like Mykola Sumtsov, Fedir Vovk and Volodymyr Yastrebov. He had a rather multifaceted career and many interests: writing, folklore, ethnography and dialectology. He closely cooperated with many active ethnographers as well as scholars of other fields, poets and writers, many of whom were members of the secret political society, Kyrylo-Mefodiyivske Bratstvo [The Brotherhood of Saints Cyril and Methodius]. One of the goals of the Brotherhood, which existed for only about a year (December 1845 – March 1847), was creating an equal opportunity for all Slavic nations to preserve and develop their national language and culture. Betrayed by a scoundrel, the Brotherhood was banned and its members were arrested and sentenced to imprisonment or exile. It is believed that Matviy Nomys avoided the fate of his friends only because his name failed to be mentioned during the proceedings (Paziak 1993, p. 9). Matviy Nomys maintained years' long connection with some of the Brotherhood members, including Taras Shevchenko (1814–1861), Panteleimon Kulish (1819–1897) and Opanas Markovych (1822–1867), whose collection of proverbs constituted the major part of the famous publication (Nomys 1864). Matviy Nomys passed away in 1900 in Lubny. He left his estate to various charitable organisations of Lubny county and to the Shevchenko Scientific Society (Struk 1993).

Vasyl Horlenko

Vasyl Horlenko (1853–1907) was born into an ancient Ukrainian family, which included such famous members as kozaks Lazar, Dmytro and Yakym Horlenko. The stories and legends about his relatives, renowned warriors, became a reason for Horlenko's fascination with the Ukrainian antiquity and its heritage (Kozar 2007, p. 211). Having obtained his initial education in Poltava and Nizhyn, Ukraine, he then studied at Sorbonne University, France. A good command of the French language and a flair for writing created an opportunity for him to work for a French newspaper, *Le Figaro*, (Rudynska 1927, 306). Vasyl Horlenko returned from Western Europe in 1880 and from 1882 he almost entirely dedicated himself to ethnographical research and writing on various aspects of Ukrainian culture. Vasyl Horlenko organised and undertook a number of ethnographic expeditions, and Mykola Kostomarov (1817–1885) accompanied him on two such expeditions (Horlenko 1886).

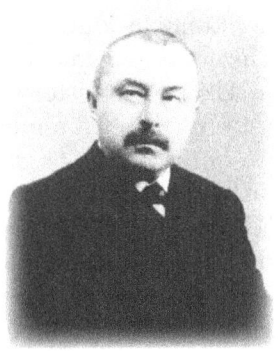

Vasyl Horlenko.

Vasyl Horlenko was a generous contributor and a great supporter of *Kievskaya Starina* [Kyivan Antiquity], where he published 76 articles (Rudynska 1927, 308). An extract of his article 'Skarzhynska's museum in Lubny' (Horlenko 1890) is included in the present compilation (see page 111).

In addition to ethnography Vasyl Horlenko's three other passions were Ukrainian fine art, theatre and literature. He diligently followed the development of these branches of art and wrote numerous reviews of new works. Vasyl Horlenko died alone in Saint Petersburg, Russia. He was buried in his native Yaroshivka village, (presently Ukrainske village, Talalaivka district, Chernihiv region, Ukraine).

Kievskaya Starina

The articles assembled in this publication were initially published in a Ukrainian journal *Kievskaya Starina* [Kyivan Antiquity] (1882–1907). The journal is a valuable source of information for those interested in Ukrainian history, literature, ethnography, archaeology and other aspects of the Ukrainian country study.

Kievskaya Starina [Kyivan Antiquity] was published in Kyiv. In the last year of its existence the name of the journal was changed to *Ukraina* [Ukraine] and the language of its publication became Ukrainian. In the previous years the journal was published almost exclusively in the Russian language since Kyiv as well as a larger part of modern Ukraine was at the time under the rule of the Russian Empire. Since the Russian Imperial government exploited a number of measures to subdue any manifestations of the Ukrainians' national identity and the national language was one of its targets, the use of the Ukrainian language was progressively banned by several legal instruments, including *Valuev Circular* (1862) and the subsequent *Ems Decree* (1876). Notwithstanding that the articles in the journal were mostly published in Russian, editors of the journal managed to include many which embraced the Ukrainian cultural identity (Kozar 2016, p. 69).

The journal's founders and contributors included a number of well-known Ukrainian scholars and public figures. A few of them are mentioned in this Foreword. Other scholars who to a larger or lesser degree were connected with the journal included Feofan Lebedyntsev (1828–1888), Mykhailo Drahomanov (1841–1895), Oleksandr Potebnia (1835–1891), Volodymyr Antonovych (1834–1908), Mykola Kostomarov (1817–1885) and Pavlo Zhytetskyi (1837–1911).

1891   Pysanky

Mykola Sumtsov

Mykola Sumtsov, a renowned Ukrainian ethnographer, published this article on pysanky in Kievskaya Starina *[Kyivan Antiquity] in 1891 – the first part in issue no. 5 and the second part in the following issue no. 6. Although he published an earlier overview in 1889 – extracted here in the chapter 'Ritual egg' – this work is positioned first since it is the most comprehensive out of all the works offered in the compilation.*

Pysanky in ancient and modern ethnography

In Western Europe scholarly studies on *pysanky* date back to the late 17th century. In 1682, in his essay *Dissertatio de Ovis Paschalibus, von Ostereiern*, which was published in Heidelberg, Arztes Johannes Richier suggested ancient Greek origins of the *pysanka* (Richier 1682). In his description of the German customs involving Easter eggs, he noted that on Easter eve adults would bury dyed eggs in the ground and then would show them to children and tell them that the eggs had been laid there by hares; furthermore, these eggs received a specific name: 'Haseneier'.

Köber, in his *Dissertatio de Ovo Paschali* (Leipzig, 1690),[1] expressed an opinion of *pysanka* having Christian Church origins. Tobiae Kraskii held the same view (Kraskii 1705). Kraskii saw *pysanka* as a symbol of the future resurrection of

1. It is likely that there is a mistake in the reference and that the author meant Johann Friedrich Köber's *Dissertatiuncula de Ovo, Quod Vocant, Paschali* (Köber 1672).

2. It seems that the original publication of the article contains a mistake in the reference's date. It is likely that the author meant the work of Johann Friedrich Gottlieb Erdmann's *Commentatio Critica de Ovo Paschali* (Erdmann 1736).

3. The author refers to the most popular colour of *krashanky* – red.

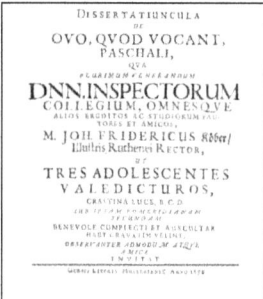

(Köber 1672).

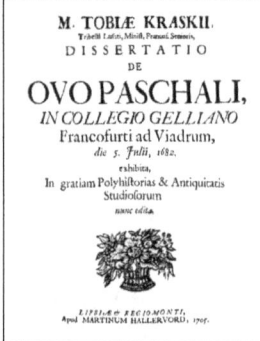

(Kraskii 1705).

the dead. His book contains references to some folk customs, such as the 'rolling' of *pysanky*. Erdmann in 1705[2] (Erdmann 1736) and Jensen in 1706 (Lauterbach & Jensen 1706) wrote about Easter eggs along the same lines. The latter asserted that the *krashanka* symbolised blood spilled by the Saviour for the sake of mankind.[3]

The contemporary writings of German scholars which relate to Easter eggs include *Das Heidenthum und dessen Bedeutung für das Christenthum* [Paganism and its importance for Christianity] by Johann Sepp (Sepp 1853), *Das Christliche Kirchenjahr* [The Christian Church Year] by Gottlob Wunderlich (Wunderlich 1884) and *Hessische Volks-Sitten und Gebräuche im Lichte der heidnischen Vorzeit* [Hessian Folk Customs and Traditions in the Light of Pagan Antiquity] by Wilhelm Kolbe (Kolbe 1888). These scholars held the view that the *pysanka* originated in Pagan antiquity, and once upon a time served as a symbol of the spring sun (Zibrt 1890). Currently the interest in *pysanka* within German scholarly circles has stalled. In the 17th century they found it necessary to devote a special study to *pysanka*, whereas in the 18th and 19th centuries they mention *pysanka* only in passing, when discussing other customs associated with the folk calendar.

In the Russian Empire – with the exception of the 17th century, when the foreign travellers Olearius and Beauplan (1651) mentioned *pysanky* in their travel accounts – Easter eggs drew attention for the first time only in the late 1870s. Fedir Vovk's article (Vovk 1878, p. 318 & p. 325) includes brief notes on the ornamentation of *pysanky*. In 1876 Olha Kosach's book entitled *Ukrainskiy Narodnyi Ornament: Vyshyvki, Tkani, Pysanky* [Ukrainian Folk Ornament: Embroidery, Fabrics and Pysanky] was published. There is a note about the ornamentation of *pysanky* in the preface (Kosach 1876, pp. 13–14), as well as 23 colour images (see page 50) which are contained in its appendix. In 1882, Oskar Kolberg made some interesting remarks about the *Galician Rus* [Halychyna or Galicia, Ukraine] *pysanky* (Kolberg 1882). In 1887 there were short articles by Bartels about Ukrainian *pysanky* in *Zeitschrift fur Ethnologie* [Journal of Ethnology] and about Polish ones in the *Wisła* journal. Two monographs on *pysanky* came out this year: in the Polish language on Polish *pysanky* by Udziela (1888) and a more extensive work in the Czech language on Moravian *pysanky* entitled *Moravske ornamenty* [Moravian ornaments] that included the articles by Jindřich Wankel and Františka Stranecka (Havelkova 1888). The Czech publication includes an extensive addendum with drawings of *pysanky*. The article of Wankel (Wankel 1888), a famous archaeologist, presented solid research on the archaeological significance of *pysanky*.

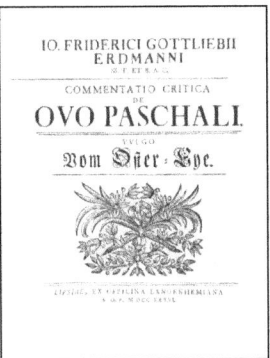

(Erdmann 1736).

In recent years the ethnographers of all Slavic countries, but mostly Polish ethnographers, have expressed a great interest in *pysanky*. In 1889, in issue no. 76 of *Kharkovskie Hubernskie Vedomosti* [Kharkiv Provincial News], I addressed the public with an appeal for information on *pysanky* to be delivered to me by way of a survey that consisted of eight paragraphs, which I offered therein. My article was later reprinted in whole and in part in the following periodicals: *Elisavetgradskiy Vesnik* [Elysavethrad Herald], *Volyn, Kievskaya Starina* [Kyivan Antiquity] and *Etnograficheskoe Obozrenie* [Ethnographic Review]. The same year, independently from my appeal to the public, in issue no. 328 of the Polish illustrated *Tygodnik* and in other illustrated Polish editions, a request to the public

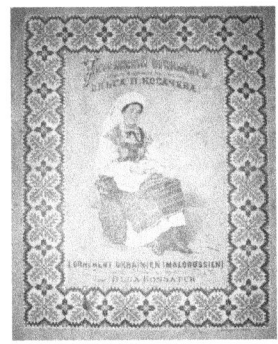

(Kosach 1876).

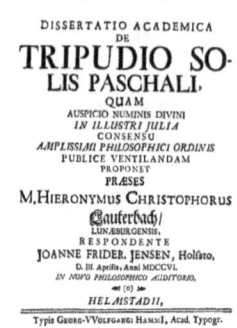

(Lauterbach & Jensen 1706).

4. Rezultat wypadl nadspodziewanie swietnie. – Pol., 'the result was surprisingly great'.

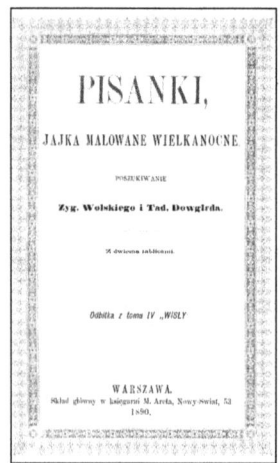

(Wolski & Dowgird 1890).

appeared regarding gathering and delivering *pysanky* as well as information about them. The request was signed by two young Polish academics, the ethnographer Zygmunt Wolski and archaeologist Tadeusz Dowgird, with the inclusion of a brief explanation and four photographs of *pysanky*, three of which were Polish and one Ukrainian. At the end of 1889, in a new Serbian magazine *Glasnik Zemaljskog Muzeja Bosne i Hercegovine* [Herald of the National Museum of Bosnia and Herzegovina], Mr Svitlic reported that Mihailo Valtrovich collects Serbian and Bosnian *pysanky* in order to study their ornamentation (Svitlic 1889, p. 60).

Among all these appeals to the educated public the most fruitful one appeared to be the Polish appeal. In issue no. 4 of *Tygodnik* and a little later in *Wisła* supplement Z. Wolski and T. Dowgird (1890) reported that they had received a few dozen descriptions and 2800 specimens of *pysanky* from 220 villages from various areas of Poland and the Right-bank Ukraine. The gatherers themselves were surprised by the success of their appeal to the society and noted that 'rezultat wypadl nadspodziewanie swietnie'.[4] The interesting fact is that the largest number of collections have been given by the provinces with predominantly or entirely Ukrainian population: Podillia – 13, Kyiv – 5, Volyn – 4 and Siedlce province – 6, whereas Warsaw – 3, Suwalki – 2, Piotrkow, Kalisz and Plock – 1 specimen each.

In 1890 *Wisła* published a brief account by Mrs Sadowska about *pysanky* in the Novominsk district of Warsaw province (Sadowska 1890) as well as a short article by T. Dowgird on *pysanka*-making methods in Poland and the distinctive features of the ornamentation of the Easter eggs (1890, book 4) (see page 38 and page 39).

Issue 15 of *Tygodnik Ilustrowany Dla*

Dzieci [Illustrated Weekly for Children] in 1889 published Udziela's account of *Galician Rus* [Halychyna or Galicia, Ukraine] *pysanky* in Pokuttia, which was accompanied by 48 drawings.

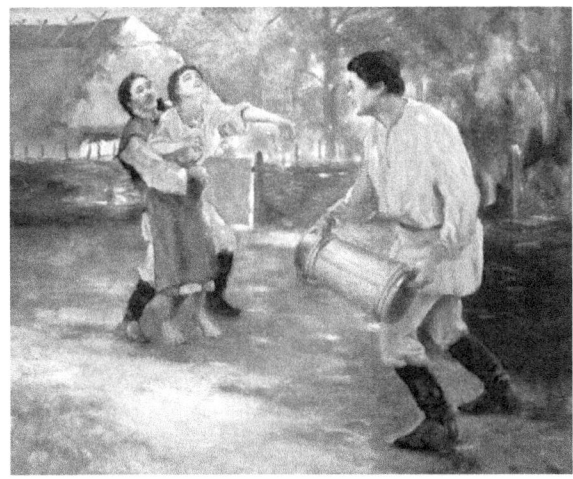

'Oblyvanyi Ponedilok'
[Pouring Monday]
by Yaroslav Pstrak
(beginning of the 20th
century).

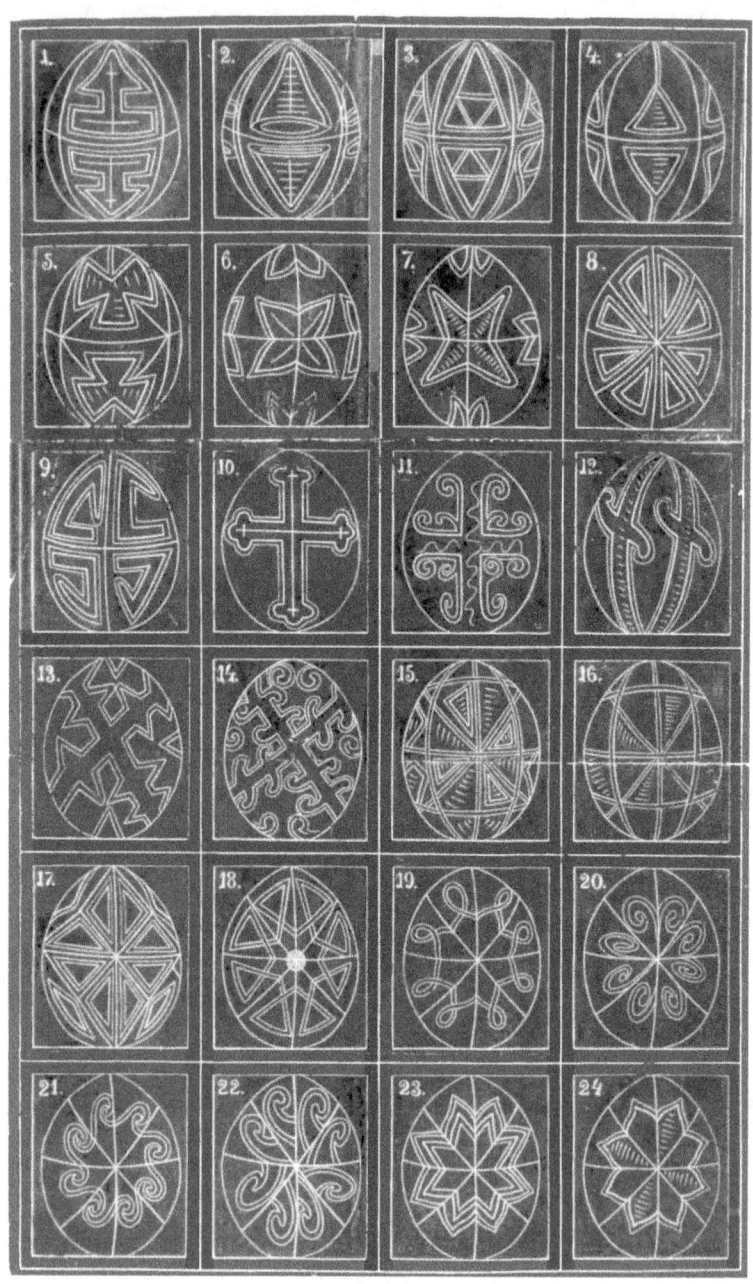

Illustrations of pysanky (Wolski & Dowgird 1890, p. 7).

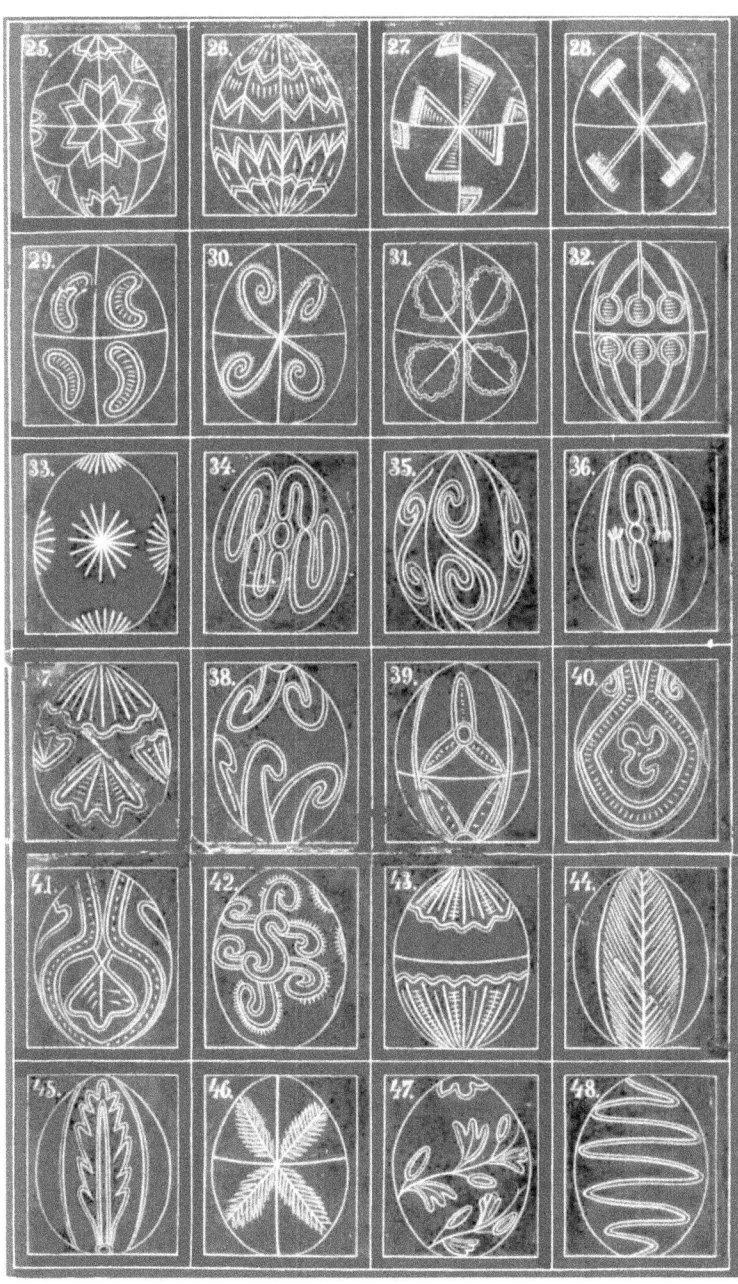

Illustrations of pysanky (Wolski & Dowgird 1890, p. 8).

Materials used in preparation of this article

We will refer to other bibliographical sources throughout the text where appropriate. However, there are only a few such sources, since the literature on the subject is extremely poor. Most of the materials that I have gathered consist of written information and of the collections of *pysanky* that were graciously sent to me by the enthusiasts of the native ethnography from several *Southern Rus* [Ukrainian] regions.

I received information on *pysanky* from the following people: 1) Fr Izmail Dmytriev, 2) D. L. Hlynskyi, 3) I. I. Manzhura, 4) M. P. Savyniv, 5) NN (via P. V. Ivanov), 6) M. D. Skubak, 7) V. N. Svet, 8) D. Pelykhov, 9) A. A. Sklobynska, 10) OV, 11) I. A. Karlovych, 12) Mr Patera (from Prague), 13) Z. Wolski, 14) Fr Fedir Rodkevych (via M. P. Savyniv), 15) Mr Stepaniv, 16) Mrs O. Proskura, 17) Mr Dontsov, 18) Mr Tovpekyn, 19) Mr Zhukov, 20) Mr Dudok, 21) Mr Myshniv, 22) Mr Lapushniak, 23) Mr Andreev, 24) Mr Rosavskyi, 25) Mr P. S., 26) Mr Prasolov, 27) Mr Druzhynin, 28) Mr Trofymovskyi, 29) V. Kobeliatskyi and 30) E. Baranovska. The information covers mainly such regions as Podillia, Volyn, Katerynoslav, Kyiv, Kharkiv and Kuban province.

My *pysanky* collection amounted to the following:

5 *pysanky* – from Mr Savyniv, Ostroverhivka village, Kharkiv county, Kharkiv province; 4 *pysanky* – purchased on the spot in Korotych village [Kharkiv county, Kharkiv province]; 1 *pysanka* – from student Bobyn, Zmiiv county; 1 *pysanka* – from student Bobyn, Izium county; 4 *pysanky* – from student Bobyn, Krasnokutsk town, Bohodukhiv county; 6 *pysanky* – P. V. Ivanov, Kupyansk town; 17 professionally made, 20 semi-professionally made and 14 amateur *pysanky* (purchased on

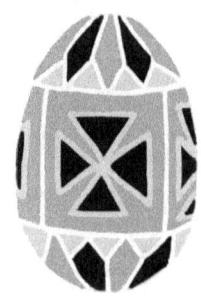

'Khrestyk' [diminutive form of 'khrest' (cross)] pysanka (Kulzhynskyi 1899, table 5, no. 14).

the spot at Okhtyrka county); and 36 *pysanky* from Fr Izmail Dmytriev, Lebedyn county.

16 *pysanky* – from student Bobyn, Katerynoslav province.

7 *pysanky* – from P. I. Petrushevskyi, Poltava county, Poltava province.

45 *pysanky* – from D. L. Hlynskyi, Hulcha village, Ostroh county, Volyn province.

37 *pysanky* – from Fr Rodkevych, Kamianets-Podilskyi province.

16 *pysanky* – from E. Baranovska, Kuban region.

3 *pysanky* – from Mr Boltenkov, Vorobjevka village, Kursk county, Kursk province.

4 *pysanky* – from M. E. Khalanskyi, Shchigry county, Kursk province.

6 wooden *pysanky* – from M. P. Savyniv, Vologda province.

1 monk *pysanka* – from Bulgaria.

***

I express my deep gratitude to all my colleagues and correspondents named in the list above.

The press have also published information on other *pysanky* collections, namely:

Z. Wolski's and T. Dowgird's collection in Warsaw. The collection is very extensive and valuable. It is exhibited in the Museum of Ethnography and contains many Ukrainian *pysanky*.

Bartels' collection in the Berlin Museum of Anthropological Society (it contains Ukrainian *pysanky*).

Collection in the Krakow Museum of Academy of Sciences.

Collection in the Museum of Science and Industry of Adrian Baraniecki in Krakow (contains many Ukrainian *pysanky*).

Collection in Count Dzieduszycki's Museum in Lviv.

Collection in the Technical Museum in Lviv.

Collection in the Brno Museum, Moravia.

Collection in the Naprstke Museum in Prague.

Mrs Kosach's collection in Kyiv.

Mr Pavlyn's collection (*Galician Rus* [Halychyna or Galicia, Ukraine] *pysanky*).

Collection in K. Skarzhynska's Museum in Lubny (consists of about 300 *pysanky*).

M. Yanchuk's collection in Moscow.

Reflections on the ancient symbolism of the egg in the folk tales

Long before Christianity, the ancient civilised peoples endowed eggs with considerable ritual-religious and symbolic significance, both in their beliefs and in their everyday life, as a symbol of the sun, which was ranked supreme in their Pagan cults. Honouring of the egg was warranted by the concept of spring's rebirth of the sun, and with it, of all the creative forces of nature.

One of the folk tale zoomorphic images of the sun is the *firebird* character, which is a bird that illuminates a large garden with one of its feathers. A wizard ('Winter Cold') kidnaps the *firebird*. However, prior to the kidnapping the *firebird* has managed to lay a golden egg, which then becomes a new source of life, light and warmth. With its hot beams the sun-egg warms the cold winter clouds, disperses fog, and forces the clouds to pour streams of rain upon earth; and thus the summer again reigns on earth.

Folk tales depicting eggs as a source of life, and as the universe, are popular among peoples both ancient and modern, both savage and civilised. Eggs were used as gifts to mark the beginning of the new year. They were praised in the divine hymns. Iron statues of eggs were placed in temples (Uspenskiy 1818, p. 643). Some would bury an egg at the place where they were going to build a city. This custom was used as the foundation for a legend about Naples being built on an egg (Voevodskyi 1874, p. 3).

Religious and symbolic meaning and ritual use of dyed eggs in the ancient cults

Ancient Egyptians viewed the egg as Kneph's attribute. The image of this deity was depicted as a hybrid, with the head of a hawk holding an egg in his mouth. That egg gave origin to fire (Uspenskiy 1818, p. 642). The egg was also an attribute of the Egyptian Sun deity, Ptah. On one of the surviving bas-reliefs Ptah is shown holding an egg, and an explanatory note located beneath indicates that the egg represents the sun. Another note says that Ptah rolls his egg in the sky (Roslavskyi-Petrovskyi 1865–69, vol. 1, p. 61).

An Indian legend about the creation of the world discusses the golden egg that floats on the water; in other words, the sun floating on the ocean of air (Afanasyev 1869, vol. 1, p. 535).

Greek and Roman philosophers, following the folk outlook, traced the origin of the universe from the egg (*ab ovo*[5]). According to the legend, which Herodotus recorded, the world was created from an egg that was laid by the fabled Phoenix in Helios' sanctuary. These classic tales found their reflection in Byzantine literature. One manuscript records the 'testimony' of John of Damascus regarding the egg as follows: "Heaven and earth are similar to an egg in every way – the eggshell is like the sky, the membrane is like the clouds, the egg white is like water and the egg yolk is like the earth." (Afanasyev 1869, vol. 1, p. 536).

Romans dyed eggs and used them in various games and ceremonies, which is evidenced by Juvenal, Ovid and Pliny the Elder. Plutarch offered an explanation of the egg depicting the all-inclusive creator (Uspenskiy 1818, p. 642).

Cornelis de Bruijn, who travelled through Persia in 1704, said that on the occasion of New Year (20 May) the Persians greeted each

5. *Ab ovo* – Lat., 'from the beginning, the egg'.

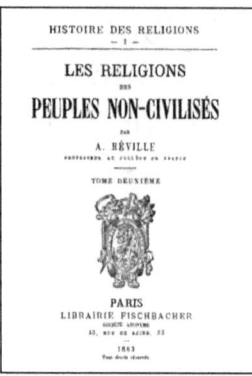

(Reville 1883).

6. Kalevala – the author refers to the edition of *The Kalevala* translated into Russian by Eduard Granstrem, with 1881 as a likely publication date (Granstrem 1881), which was the first prose presentation of the epic.

other with gifts of multi-coloured dyed eggs (Uspenskiy 1818, p. 641).

In Polynesian mythology the visible world is personified by a bird, a form taken by the creator of the world, the god Tangaroa. In other accounts, Tangaroa originated from the egg. Polynesian islands were formed from the breakage of the egg (Reville 1883, vol. 2, p. 25). In one of the versions (from the islands of Samoa) there was only sky originally, whereas the earth was covered with water. Tangaroa sent his daughter to the earth in the form of a Snipe bird. She found sharp cliffs that were jutting out over the sea, and sowed soil and plants there (Christmann & Oberländer 1873).

Remarkably, a similar tale about the creation of the world is present in the Finnish Kalevala[6] (Lönnrot, E. 1835–36). The Mother of the Waters, Ilmatar, initially lived in air; then she descended to the ocean that covered all the land. For 700 years she rocked on its waves. A wild duck mistook Ilmatar's knee for land and built a nest on it and laid one iron and six golden eggs. Ilmatar jerked, the eggs broke and fell into the sea. The whole visible world originated from these eggs: the earth from the bottom part; the sky from the top part; the sun from the yolk; and the moon from the egg white.

The beliefs and legends of the Slavic peoples preserved many remnants of this world-wide cosmogonic approach. Folk tales on the subject of the origin of the world from an egg are recorded by Poles (Petrow 1878, p. 125), Czechs (Stranecka 1888, p. 8) and Carantanians (Afanasyev 1869, vol. 1, p. 531), and in various locations of the Russian Empire. The Russian folk tales based on this motif, as with similar Slavic tales, substitute different main elements by taking a subdued cosmogonic approach: a town, fairgrounds and so on come out from an egg, instead of the sun, moon and earth. In a Ukrainian folk tale about the first century of creation, a mouse and a sparrow are dividing millet between themselves and they start to fight. Animals opposed the birds, but the birds defeated the animals. Man helped the birds. As a reward he received an egg, in which a kingdom was concealed[7] (Kulish 1856–57, vol. 2, p. 31). In the Belarusian folk tales, a hero acquired golden, silver and copper eggs (an example of a traditional trinity), which he then threw to the ground, and golden, silver and copper palaces appeared from the eggs (Romanov 1887, pp. 84–85).

As a version of these folk tales one can consider those many tales where life and death are hidden in the egg. In the Russian folk tales, the life of *Kosh (Koshchey) Bessmertnyi* is hidden in an egg, which is hidden in a duck and the duck is hidden in a locked trunk. *Ivan Tsarevych* acquired and broke the egg, and then *Kosh Bessmertnyi* died (Sadovnikov 1884, p. 201). In the Belarusian tales, the death of *Koshchey* is in an egg, the egg is in the bird, the bird is in the nest, which is on the stone, which is under an oak tree, which is on an island (Romanov 1887, p. 72). Analogous storylines are found in Indian (Minaev 1876), French (Cosquin 1886), Sicilian (Gonzenbach 1870, vol. 2, p. 215) and Zulu (Koropchevskiy (ed.) 1874, p. 64) tales. Similar stories constitute part of *Kalilag and Damnag*[8] and resemble one of the ancient Egyptian tales (Maspero 1882, p. 182).

Evidence that *pysanky* represent the Sun are also found in the games played by youths during the Bright Week celebrations as well as in their ornamentation – but there will be more discussion of games later.

A legend about the origin of the custom to use red-dyed eggs at Easter survived in Greece,

---

7. In P. Kulish's *Notes on Southern Rus*, the folk tale is entitled 'Myth about the first century of creation'.

8. *Kalilag and Damnag* – is a Syrian translation of *Panchatantra*, the ancient Indian collection of animal fables. The author refers to an edition translated into Russian by M. O. Attay and M. V. Riabinin (with 1889 as a likely publication date), namely, p. 154.

where the founder of the custom is Saint Mary Magdalene. After the Saviour's ascension into heaven, Saint Mary Magdalene went to Rome to preach the Gospels. She appeared before the Emperor Tiberius, offered him a red egg and said: "Christ is risen!" This was the beginning of her preaching. When the first Christians learnt about this offering by Saint Mary Magdalene, they started to imitate her and give each other eggs. While studying a 10th century manuscript, which was located in Saint Athanasius monastery (near Thessaloniki), Constantine Oikonomos (a Greek scholar of the 1830s) discovered a citation mentioning the existence of *krashanky* since the apostolic times, as a tradition originated by Saint Mary Magdalene (Kalinskiy 1877 p. 461).

This belief is also known in Ukraine. Recently the following story was recorded in Tarasivka village, Kupyansk county, in the province of Kharkiv: 'Mary Magdalene went to the Lord's tomb but did not find him there. An angel proclaimed that Christ was risen. It frightened and gladdened her and she ran home. There she saw dyed eggs and said "Christ is risen!" She took those eggs, and as soon as she came out of the house, she saw the Apostles walking towards her. Filled with joy, she began to give them eggs saying: "Christ is risen" and they kissed each other, rejoicing. By God's design, man's every step has its purpose: she was giving eggs because she had nothing else, and as it happens, an egg is dead but a live chicken comes out of it; likewise, Christ was dead but he gifted life to us.'

In Poltava province S. Rudanskyi recorded the following wonderful story about the origin of *krashanky*: 'One poor man was carrying eggs to the town to sell, while at the same time the Lord was taken to the place of his crucifixion. When the cross, which the Lord was carrying, fell down, the poor man felt sorry for him. He put down his basket and helped the Lord to carry his cross. After helping, he returned to his basket and saw that all his eggs had became *krashanky* and *pysanky*.' (Drahomanov 1876, p. 145).

Two other versions of an explanation of the origin of Easter eggs were recorded in Arapovka village, Kupyansk county. According to one interpretation, *pysanky* are made in commemoration of the tortures that were suffered by the Saviour. His torturers 'popysaly'[9] his whole body (i.e. flogged him with whips). According to another story, 'When Jesus Christ rose from the dead, he told the sentry who guarded his tomb, "Go and tell all: 'Christ is risen!' And in order for them to believe you, here have this sign", and he gave them a *krashanka* each, which he had brought from his tomb.'

Still other explanations on the subject are recorded in Zelenchukska village, Kuban region: 1) the eggs are dyed red because of the blood that came out when Jesus Christ's ribs were perforated; 2) the eggs are dyed in memory of the beheading of John the Baptist, because when his head was brought to Herod, Herod blushed with shame and pity, and since then even fruit has begun to blush.

The following version is recorded in Bzhedukhivska village [Kuban region]: 'Once, on the first day of Easter celebrations, a Christian met a Jewish acquaintance, who was returning from the market, where he had bought some fresh chicken eggs. The Christian offered the Jewish acquaintance to *khrystosuvatysia* [to have a ritual exchange of Easter greetings], but the latter declined, giving his reason for refusal that he had no *krashanky* to exchange, according to the Christian tradition.

"But what is it in your headscarf? It seems, there are eggs," the Christian said.

"Yes, they are eggs," the latter replied. "However, they are fresh and not dyed."

In order to assure the Christian of that, he lifted his parcel, but when he looked inside, he saw that the white fresh eggs had turned into *pysanky*. Having recovered from his astonishment, the Jewish man exchanged Easter greetings with the Christian and decided to be baptised.'

In Kharkiv I have heard the following story. A Jewish man did not believe it when he was told that Christ had been resurrected. "I will believe in it," he said, pointing at the eggs, "when these white eggs turn red." Immediately, the eggs turned into *krashanky*. This story is an alteration of a very common motif about a resurrected rooster[10] (Potebnia 1883–87, vol. 2, p. 765). Francis Child's collection of English

9. 'Popysaly' – is a Ukrainian verb, past tense of 'popysaty', Ukr., 'to have written'. Here, the verb is used as a slang that refers to marks left by whips after flogging. This story is based on the theory that the word *'pysanka'* is derived from 'pysaty' (Ukr., 'to write' or 'to draw').

10. The *koliadka* in Oleksandr Potebnia's monograph is entitled 'LXXXII. Resurrection. A Rooster that was brought back to life.' The *koliadka* is about a girl telling her father that she saw God who rose from the dead. Her father does not believe her. As a proof in support of her story, a rooster, that has been roasted, comes back to life and starts crowing.

11. One-Sided Fish

(Dudari village, Kaniv county)

Well, they say that it was on Saturday when Archangel Gabriel appeared before the Mother of God and said, "Your son will be raised from the dead." At that moment the Mother of God was eating fish; and she has already eaten its flesh and only bones were left [on one of its sides]. She crossed herself and said, "Only then my son will be raised from the dead, when this fish becomes alive again." Suddenly, the fish – 'splash'... became alive.

***

I do not know whether you have ever seen that fish, but I saw it with my own eyes in the Dniester River. On its one side it looks completely alive, but on its other side there are only bones as if all the flesh from them has been eaten clean – and that was the way it was moving – on its one side.

(Chubynskyi 1872–78, vol. 1, p. 67).

and Scottish ballads lists numerous Western European versions of this motif (Child 1882–98). Legends on the subject also include a Ukrainian legend about a lopsided fish (from Kaniv county), which is mentioned in Chubynskyi's *Works* (Chubynskyi 1872–78, vol. 1, p. 67).[11]

Poles in Siedlce province say that those stones that were used to kill Saint Stephen, the first martyr, were turned into *pysanky*, and nowadays *pysanky* are made in memory of that event (Ulanowska 1884, p. 294). Another Polish legend on the origin of *pysanky* is recorded in Ripchytsi village: a group of Jewish people who wished to persuade Pontius Pilate to pass the death sentence on Jesus gifted Pilate's children with dyed eggs (Udziela 1888, p. 4).

Legends about the origin of *pysanky* are rarely encountered. For the most part, the peasants do not offer a reason for the custom. "The most comprehensive of my questioning," one priest wrote to me, "among the most astute of the common folk in my parish resulted in no sought-after information. These individuals gave the same answer: 'It has been like this since long ago.'

Besides those religious tales on the origin of *pysanky* already mentioned, it seems that no other manifestations on this account exist in literature, with the exception, perhaps, of a few proverbs like: 'She complains of poor health, but looks as pretty as *pysanka*' (Kupyansk county).

The *pysanky's* common names are defined by their colour and the methods by which they are made.

'*Krashanky*' is the term used by Ukrainians, Poles and Russians for those eggs that are dyed in a single colour with no ornament. '*Krashanky*' also encompasses eggs that are dyed with a 'wood' or 'marble' effect. In Katerynoslav province, all the eggs, even the wild birds' eggs, are called *krashanky*; for instance, 'a sparrow *krashanka*' or 'great bustard *krashanka*' and so on. This expanded meaning of the word '*krashanka*' derived from the fact that Ukrainians of Katerynoslav province consider the word 'yaytse' [egg] to be indecent.[12] If anyone accidentally mentions the word in polite company, he or she will become embarrassed while those present stare at him in astonishment, as if they have heard something vulgar. The red Easter egg is called the 'red *krashanka*'.

Folk names of krashanky and pysanky

12. 'Yaytse' – [Ukr., 'egg], the author refers to the fact that one of the meanings of the word 'yaytse' in the Ukrainian language as slang is 'testicle'.

***

'*Pysanky*' – is the term used by Ukrainians, Russians and Poles for those eggs that have two, three or more colours.

'Piski' – is a regional Polish name for '*pysanky*' (Tarnow city).

'Halunky' – is a Ukrainian name for '*krashanky*', used in Kamianets-Podilskyi province, from the word 'halun' [Engl., 'alum'].

'Malowanki' – is Polish for '*krashanky*'.

'Rysowanki' and 'byczki' – are regional Polish names for '*pysanky*' and '*krashanky*'.

'Skrobanki' – are Polish '*pysanky*', where the ornamentation has been carved with a needle or knife.

'Kraslice' – is a Czech or Moravian name for '*krashanky*' and '*pysanky*'.

'Pirh' – is a Carinthian name for '*krashanky*' and '*pysanky*'.

'Margučiai' – is a name for coloured eggs in Lithuania.

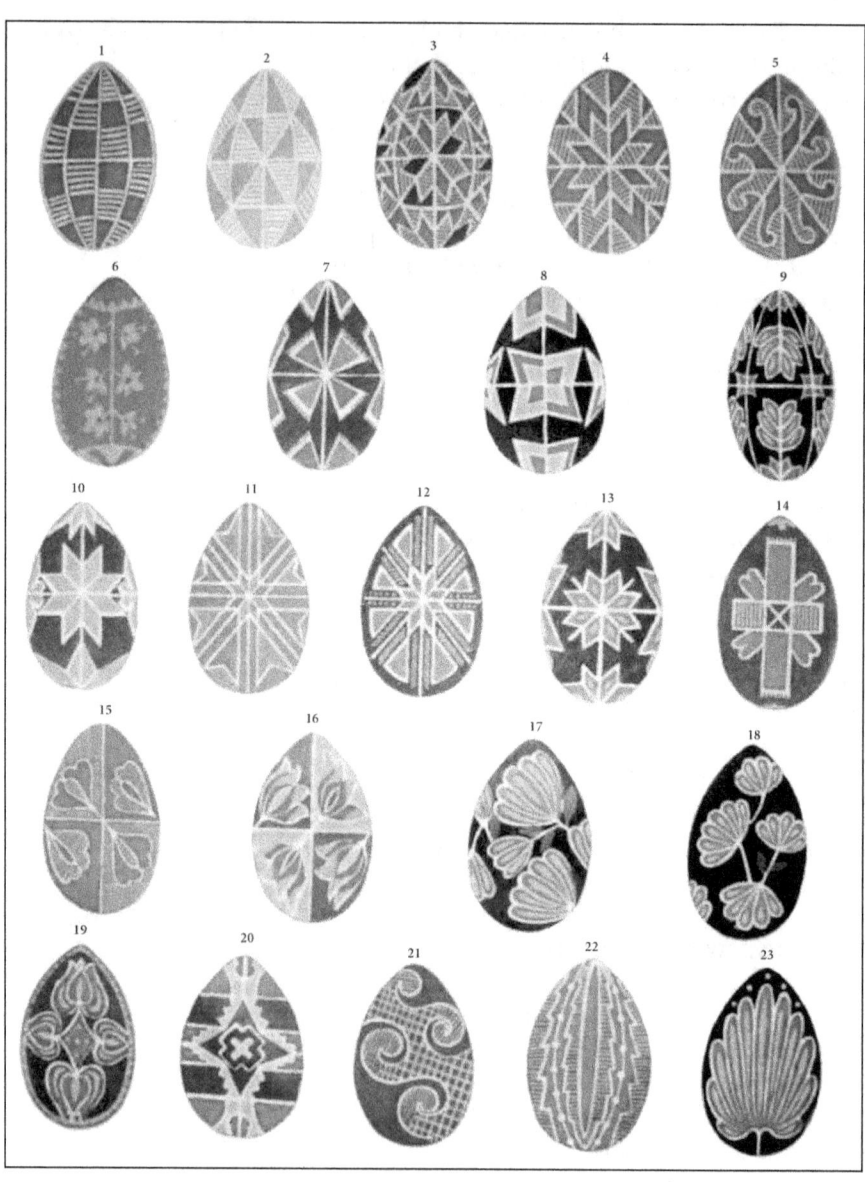

Illustrations of pysanky (Kosach 1876).

Although at one stage *pysanky* were popular over an extensive area, over time this area became increasingly narrower and smaller. In the last century *pysanky* were known throughout Europe and in the Near East (for example, among Greeks and Persian Shias). Nowadays, they continue to be common among almost all Ukrainians (from Galicia [Halychyna] to Kuban), Poles, Czechs, Serbs, Bulgarians, Romanians, Greeks, Lithuanians and Latvians. The Russian southern provinces practise *pysanky*, whereas the northern provinces have wooden *krashanky*. In eastern Siberia, for lack of chickens, instead of *pysanky* they use the mottled eggs of wild birds, which are gathered with great difficulty from the coastline cliffs (Mazurewicz 1889). On Maundy Thursday, the Greeks of Asia Minor take as many *pysanky* to the church as there are family members in their own household. They keep these *pysanky* until Easter (Carnoy & Nicolaides 1889, p. 302). A ritual involving the use of the eggs during Bright Week was not unusual in Germany as well (Heinecke 1889, vol. 6, p. 351); some German towns still enjoy *pysanky*. In France, one-coloured (red) *krashanky* remain in use. These were exhibited at the Congress of the Folklorists in Paris in 1889[13] (Zmigrodzki 1889, p. 971).

Areas of popularity for pysanky in modern times

13. Congrés internationale des traditions populaires, Paris, 1889.

Time of pysanky's origin

The time of the origin of *pysanky* among Slavic peoples cannot be determined precisely. It is unknown whether *pysanky* were in use in [Kyivan] Rus prior to the adoption of Christianity, or whether they came here under the influence of Christianity, or whether they were brought here from the Byzantine Empire or Bulgaria. One cannot absolutely deny the pre-Christian existence of *pysanky* in Rus, taking into account the extensive use of religious rituals of the ancient Slavs involving roosters and hens. However, more probable is the assumption that the Rus *pysanky* had a Byzantine origin, which is indicated by the relevant religious myths. One can assume that they have been introduced to Rus in ancient times, along with Christianity. In the 16th and 17th centuries *pysanky* already existed in northern and southern Rus.

During Easter Week, the Muscovy tsars gave their minions goose, duck, chicken and wooden eggs, which were dyed in bright colours on a golden background. According to I. Kalinskiy, in the early days of Muscovy the Easter eggs were made by bakers, icon makers, armoury millers and the monks of Trinity Lavra of Saint Sergius (Zabelin 1862). This custom attracted the attention of foreigners who visited the state of Muscovy. It was mentioned by Herberstein, Giovio, Margeret, Petreius, Olearius and others (Tereshchenko 1848, vol. 6, p. 93). In the 18th century *pysanky* and *krashanky* were used among the upper classes of society. They say that Suvorov, after having attended Matins and early liturgy, used to stand in a row with priests and exchange Easter greetings with everyone there. Batmen standing behind Suvorov held baskets with dyed eggs while the latter handed the eggs to everyone present, but he himself did not accept eggs from people (Tereshchenko 1848, vol. 6, p. 90). Until recent

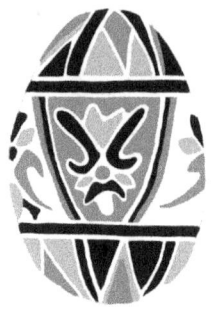

'Pavuchky' [diminutive form of 'pavuky' (spiders)] pysanka (Kulzhynskyi 1899, table 12, no. 6).

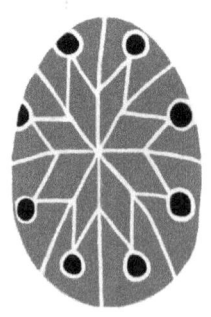

'Pavuchky' [diminutive form of 'pavuky' (spiders)] pysanka (Kulzhynskyi 1899, table 8, no. 4).

times the upper-class families continued to observe a similar custom. However, the custom to *khrystosuvatysia* [to have a ritual exchange of Easter greetings] with people who had gifted *pysanky* is now out of use among the intellectual circles of society, and *krashanky* have became just a decoration on the Easter table.

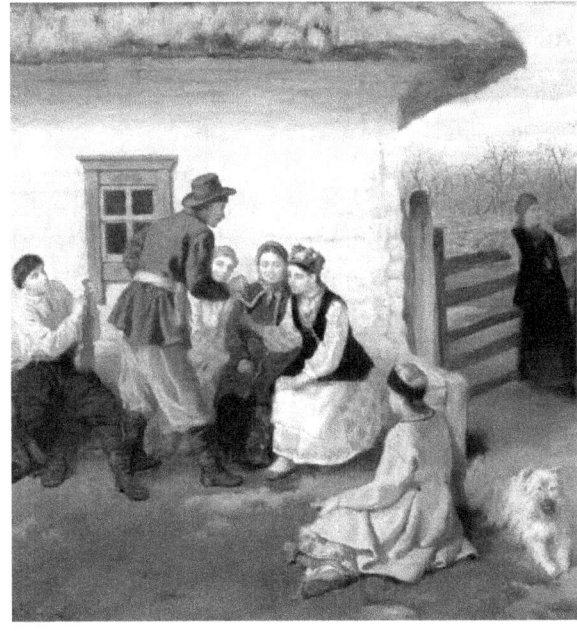

Detail of 'Easter in Ukraine' by Kostiantyn Trutovskyi (1883).

Mystical and ceremonial ambience

Guillaume Le Vasseur de Beauplan, who served in Ukraine in the middle of the 17th century, noted, among other things, that: "On Holy Saturday everyone goes to the church in order to be present at the ceremony, during which an icon of the Saviour is put in a coffin and then removed with great honours. After that, men and women, old and young, kneel down before the Bishop, and hand him eggs, dyed in red or yellow, saying, 'Christ is risen!' The Bishop, taking the eggs, answers: 'In truth, is risen!'... Metropolitan Mohyla, head of the Ukrainian bishops, performed this ritual in Kyiv in the same manner as that of the poorest village priest, who, in the Ukrainian manner, is called 'Panotets' (Engl., 'father'). For eight consecutive days, one cannot leave home without a good supply of coloured eggs, in order to *khrystosuvatysia* [to have a ritual exchange of Easter greetings] with all one's friends." (Beauplan 1651).

With few exceptions, the time for making *pysanky* falls on Holy Week Thursday, Friday and Saturday. In Starokorsunska village, Chornomorria,[14] the dyeing of the eggs necessarily begins on Maundy Thursday, when church bells chime to attend the Passion Matins. On this day, no more than ten eggs are dyed, which are then gathered in a special bundle, and they remain like that until the first day of Easter. The same custom is observed in many other places of Chornomorria. In Zelenchukska village [Kuban region] they dye eggs on Maundy Thursday and, if necessary, during the remaining two days of Holy Week; during this time, a large family will manage to paint about a hundred eggs. An identical custom exists among the Greeks of Asia Minor in the vicinity of Smyrna and in some places in Poland.

14. Chornomorria – is a territory in Kuban named after the Ukrainian kozak settlements established at the end of 18th century, when the Russian Empress Catherine II gave the Black Sea (Ukr., 'Chorne More') Kozak Host the rights to the lands that included territory on the right bank of the Kuban River.

In many places of Ukraine they begin to make *pysanky* gradually, from the beginning or from the middle of the Great Lent, whereas *krashanky* are made in the last days of Holy Week. In Barsukovska village, Kuban region, they make *krashanky* on Holy Saturday, whereas they start to make *pysanky* on the fifth week of the Great Lent. The same custom exists in Kalynove village, Kupyansk county, and in some places of Poland (Dowgird 1890, p. 824). In the northern parts of the Polish ethnographic regions they paint eggs from *Hrobky Week* to *Green Week* (Dowgird 1890, p. 824). In Tarnow city they start making *pysanky* from noon on Bright Monday until *Green Week* (Udziela 1888, p. 4). In Bosnia it takes place from Good Friday to the Feast of the Ascension (Svitlic 1889). In general, the time for *pysanka*-making is determined by economic factors.

The dyeing of the eggs on the Maundy Thursday in some areas, for example, in Huriyska village, Kuban region, is explained by the belief that if the colouring of the eggs is conducted on the Maundy Thursday, those *pysanky* and *krashanky* will not go rotten for twelve or more days, no matter where they are kept, whereas other *krashanky*, whether they are made before or after Maundy Thursday, will soon spoil and become unusable.

The colouring of the eggs is carried out exclusively by women: in some places by young women; in others, where the custom is already dying out, by a few old women. In some places, with the decline of the custom, professional artists have come onto the scene. Among the Poles (Udziela 1888, p. 5 & Sadowska 1890, p. 461) and Ukrainians of Yampil county, Kamianets-Podilskyi province, young women colour eggs. Two, three or more of them gather together in one house and merrily attend to an enjoyable task, sometimes in the presence of young men. In Kharkiv province it is mostly old women doing the job, working alone.

Pysanka-making accessories: the stylus and dyes

In experienced hands, the decorating is done swiftly and the egg is soon covered with an elegant ornament. Here is a description of the work of Maria Sukhodolova, the best master of *pysanka*-making in Hulcha village, Ostroh county: "Sukhodolova has not only informed me of the theory of her art, but also acquainted me with it in practice. She showed me all the necessary appliances of the *pysanka*-making and in my presence turned one egg into a simple *pysanka*. In doing that, Sukhodolova impressed me with the agility of her technique and her skilfulness. Drawing a rather complex pattern on a *pysanka* happened as quickly and deftly as writing by a calligrapher. Holding an egg between the thumb and forefinger of her left hand, she held a stylus in her right hand like a pen, lightly touching the eggs with her right little finger to stabilise her writing hand. The lines that came out from the stylus were completely smooth and accurate." (*Elisavetgradskiy Vesnik* [Elysavethrad Herald], 1889, no. 103).

In some places certain rituals accompany the making of *pysanky*. In the Kamianets-Podilskyi province and in Kuban region they start working on *pysanky* only after fasting. In Anyno village, Lebedyn county, a woman who is preparing to make *pysanky* washes the eggs and makes dyes from the melted snow, which she gathers in the valley and transports early in the morning, without turning back or to the side, and if she meets someone she neither greets them nor responds to any greetings or questions. In short, she observes strict silence. Here, the custom of the colouring of the eggs is connected with a belief about the mysterious and powerfully curative properties of untarnished water, a belief that is popular in Russia, Germany and France.

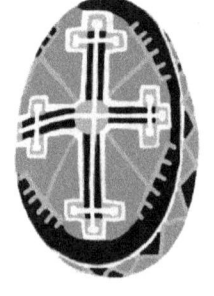

'Khresty' [crosses] pysanka (Kulzhynskyi 1899, table 9, no. 6).

In Hulcha village, Ostroh county, the eggs are kept in dye for a duration of two or three 'Our Father's'; in other words, for the time it takes to read the prayer 'Our Father' two or three times[15] (*Elisavetgradskiy Vesnik* [Elysavethrad Herald], 1889, no. 103).

There are only a few *pysanka*-making appliances: a pot of wax; a shard with hot coals, on which the wax is melted; a home-made stylus; and the dyes. These simple appliances, in particular the dyes, deserve separate attention.

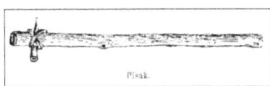

A Polish stylus, 'pisak',
(Dowgird 1890, p. 820).

15. It takes approximately 1–1.5 minutes to read 'Our Father' prayer.

Methods of pysanka-making

Dyes are either home-made or purchased. The former are extracted from plants – either local garden flora or forest flora, as follows:

Yellow dye is extracted from the wild apple tree bark, onion skin or, more rarely, elderberry flowers. The yellow dye is obtained in the following way: apple tree bark or onion skin is put in a pot and cold water is poured over it and then boiled. In Barsukovska village, Kuban region, dark-yellow or 'havana' dyes are made from the ripe onion skin, whereas pale yellow is from local serratula flowers. In Kupyansk county yellow dye is extracted from the broth of the yellow water-lily. For this purpose the Poles use the yellow flowers of *Caltha palustris* (Udziela 1888).

The dark-blue dye used in Udobna village, Kuban region, is extracted from a plant that belongs to the onion family called bluebells, which are blue in colour. This plant shows up on the surface of the ground early in spring, together with snowdrops. If the dye is re-boiled, then the eggs are dyed in dark-blue or black colours. In Katerynoslav province, they achieve indigo dye from buckwheat chaff broth, whereas in Kharkiv province it comes from the dried flowers of blue malva (*Althea rosea*).

In Kuban region the light-blue dye for *pysanky* is extracted from the spring flowering primula.

Green dye is extracted from blueberries or berries of wild elderberry, which are triturated with a solution of yellow dye into mush (in Podillia), from aspen catkins (also in Podillia), from the rye leaves (among the Poles), from the flower of dark-red malva in conjunction with yellow dye (in Kharkiv province), from scilla seedlings (Kharkiv and Katerynoslav province) and from moss (among the Poles in Warsaw province).

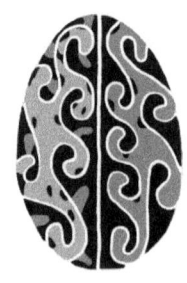

'Bezkonechnyk'
[eternity band] pysanka
(Kulzhynskyi 1899,
table 5, no. 12).

The black dye with a bluish tint, like a raven wing, is achieved from the alder bark and young tatar maple leaves (*Acer tataricum*).

The red dye in Polissia is made from local cochineal (Levchenko 1875, vol. 2, p. 149).

A marble effect is achieved by mixing the broth of dried leaves with honeycomb honey or, more often, by wrapping eggs into pieces of coloured paper or calico material.

Red and dark-blue colours, in most cases, are currently achieved from aniline dyes. In many areas fuchsine and methylene blue have replaced traditional homemade dyes due to their low cost and colour quality advantages. In some places one can hear disapproval of fuchsine. Thus, a popular belief is recorded in Kubanske village, Kuban region, that it is a sin to dye Easter eggs in fuchsine. However, no one can explain why it is a sin and, in fact, in Kubanske village fuchsine is the most commonly used dye for Easter eggs. The villagers believe fuchsine to be a toxic dye and call it 'v'yidlyva' [caustic], because the eggshell is coloured not only outside, but also on the inside, and in the case of a crack the egg white gets dyed as well. Red sandalwood dye and fuchsine are bought in shops or swapped (in Kuban region) in exchange for eggs, salo and bore bristles from dealers who visit each household.

To make *pysanky*, in addition to dyes, one needs decolourising liquid. Most often it happens to be beetroot kvas or a solution of alums.

A stylus, which is the only instrument for drawing on *pysanky*, can be a thin tin tube about a centimetre long, attached by a thread to the split ends of a small stick. The tubes are made by the craftswomen themselves from pieces of thin sheets of metal, which, in order to form the tube, they roll on a needle. The styluses used can be of various calibres, depending on the thickness of the line that is required in the *pysanka* pattern. When drawing, the tube is dipped into melted wax then the desired pattern is created with the tip of the tube. This is how the styluses are made in Ostroh county, Volyn province (*Elisavetgradskiy Vesnik* [Elysavethrad Herald], 1889, no. 103).

In Kupyansk county, Kharkiv province, styluses are made the same way using a square piece of foil (about an inch in length and 1½ in width) rolled on a needle.

In Kyslytske village, Yampil county, Kamianets-Podilskyi province, the stylus is made as follows: one of the girls pulls out an earring and breaks off a piece of 'wire' from it; that is, the metal hook that is put through the ear. This wire is tied to a wooden stick, and she proclaims: "We should draw *pysanky*!" This means that it is time to get down to business. The wire is attached or tied to the stick known as a stylus. The stylus is dipped into melted wax and wax patterns are applied to an egg.

The Polish stylus, 'pisak', is identical to the Volyn and Kharkiv ones (Dowgird 1890, p. 820) (see page 57). The Serbian 'sharalik' is similar to them as well (Svitlic 1889).

The convenience of the styluses, which are used in the Volyn and Kharkiv regions as well as in Poland, lies in the fact that wax lies on the egg evenly, in smooth lines. Earring hooks and similar instruments produce thicker lines.

In Kubanske village, Kuban region, they pour wax on the surface of the egg through a straw tube.

In some places, for example, Neberdzhaievska village, Kuban region, they hold a wax candle in a tilted position, in order for the drops of melted wax to fall from the candle, and then make various figures with it on the eggshell. This method of drawing gives no opportunity for the ornament to be refined, accurate and elegant, the properties that are characteristic to *pysanky* drawn with the styluses.

The *pysanka*-making process usually goes like this: when a pattern is done or drawn on the natural background of the eggshell colour [white], the egg is usually put first and foremost in a solution of yellow dye. Having pulled out the egg from the dye, we thus obtain a yellow background with a white pattern on it, as the dye cannot cover those places that have been covered with wax. Further ornamentation is then drawn onto the yellow background using wax and then the egg is dipped into green dye. Therefore, we end up with white and yellow patterns on a green background. More ornamentation is then drawn onto the green background using wax and then the egg is dipped into beetroot kvas for discolouration. Instead of the green background we will have the background of the natural eggshell colour. The egg is then placed into either red or blue dye, depending on the preference. You cannot put the egg into red or blue dye without first discolouring it from the previous dyes, because mixing green with red will not result in red. Similarly, mixing green and blue will not result in a dark-blue colour of the desired tone. On the other hand, it is recommended that the egg be dyed in the green immediately after the yellow, as it is the best means to make the green colour more intense and durable. With regard to discolouration, after dipping the egg into beetroot kvas, you need to wipe the egg well with a woollen cloth first, and then with a linen cloth. After an egg is painted in red dye, one can write on the red background with wax again, and so on.

Thus, the *pysanka* pattern may consist of several colours, depending on the maker's design. The *pysanka*'s background colour becomes the one in which the egg is dipped last. If the colour of the natural eggshell background is desired, then the egg is discoloured at the end. When dyeing and drawing are completed, slightly heat the egg in front of the flame to melt the wax. After the drawing on the eggs is complete, they are baked. To do that, the eggs are placed in a bowl in a not-very-hot oven for 10–15 minutes. This concludes the technical side of the matter. The described method gives *pysanky* not only a good tone of colour, but also presents them with considerable strength. As for the process of drawing itself, it requires much time, patience and dexterity.

This method of drawing eggs is found in Ukraine, Galicia and Kuban region, and among the Poles, Czechs and Bosnian Serbs.

Sometimes they resort to the following method: they dye the egg first and then engrave a pattern with a sharp needle or a knife. Lithuanians and Poles call such *pysanky* 'skrobanki'. This custom is popular among the Lithuanians in Kaunas province and Lomza county (Dowgird 1890, p. 822) and among Czech-Moravians. It is also known in Russia, which is mentioned in *Poshekhonskaya Starina* [Old Years in Poshekhonye] (Saltykov-Shchedrin 1890), and in Ukraine (see *pysanka* no. 6 in Kosach's *Ukrainskiy Narodnyi Ornament* [Ukrainian Folk Ornament] (Kosach 1876) (see page 50), where flowers are scratched on the dyed red background using a knife).

In monasteries and families of the educated society, the methods of making *pysanky* are very diverse and artistic: they glue the eggs with coloured pieces of silk fabric or pictures, they cover walnuts in wax and attach coloured threads on top of them and so on. However, we do not include a discussion of urban and monastic *pysanky* here.

The uses of krashanky and pysanky

[The original chapter heading read: "The uses of *krashanky* and *pysanky*: during the exchange of Easter greetings; in swaps or as a present; to obtain beauty and health; to assure soil fertility and the multiplying of the bees; to avoid lightning strike and fire; to cure an illness; to protect against witches and evil eye; to remember the dead; and in children's games".]

The ritual use of *krashanky* and *pysanky* occurs within the last days of Great Lent, Bright Week as well as *Hrobky Week*, and predominantly with the first days of Easter.

In Bzheduhivska village, Kuban region, when customarily honouring epitaphios on Good Friday, they lay red eggs beside it.

In Kupyansk county, Kharkiv province, one of the family members attends the reading of the Acts and Matins on the eve of Easter Sunday, keeping a *pysanka* in their pocket, which is then kept as the home amulet during the whole year. In Volyn they use *pysanky* to decorate baskets with bread, when they take them to the church to be blessed (*Elisavetgradskiy Vesnik* [Elysavethrad Herald], 1889, no. 103).

Krashanky and *pysanky* are customarily used during *rozhovyny* [first ritual meal after Great Lent] and *khrystosuvannia* [Easter greeting ritual in Ukraine]. In Ukraine, Kuban region and Galicia [Halychyna] (Lozynskyi 1859, p. 507), they begin *rozhovyny* with a blessed red egg.

In Volyn, *pysanky* are used as Easter gifts for honourable and respected persons (*Elisavetgradskiy Vesnik* [Elysavethrad Herald], 1889, no. 103).

Girls gift *pysanky* to their fiancés and sometimes vice versa – the lads present them to girls. In H. Kvitka-Osnovyanenko's novel, *Ot tobi i skarb* [Here's a treasure for you] (1837), skilful Oryshka made a good and pretty *pysanka* for her betrothed, Tymosia, a scribe's son, "the

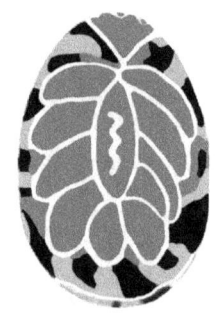

'Rybka' [diminutive form of 'ryba' (fish)] pysanka (Kulzhynskyi 1899, table 10, no. 1).

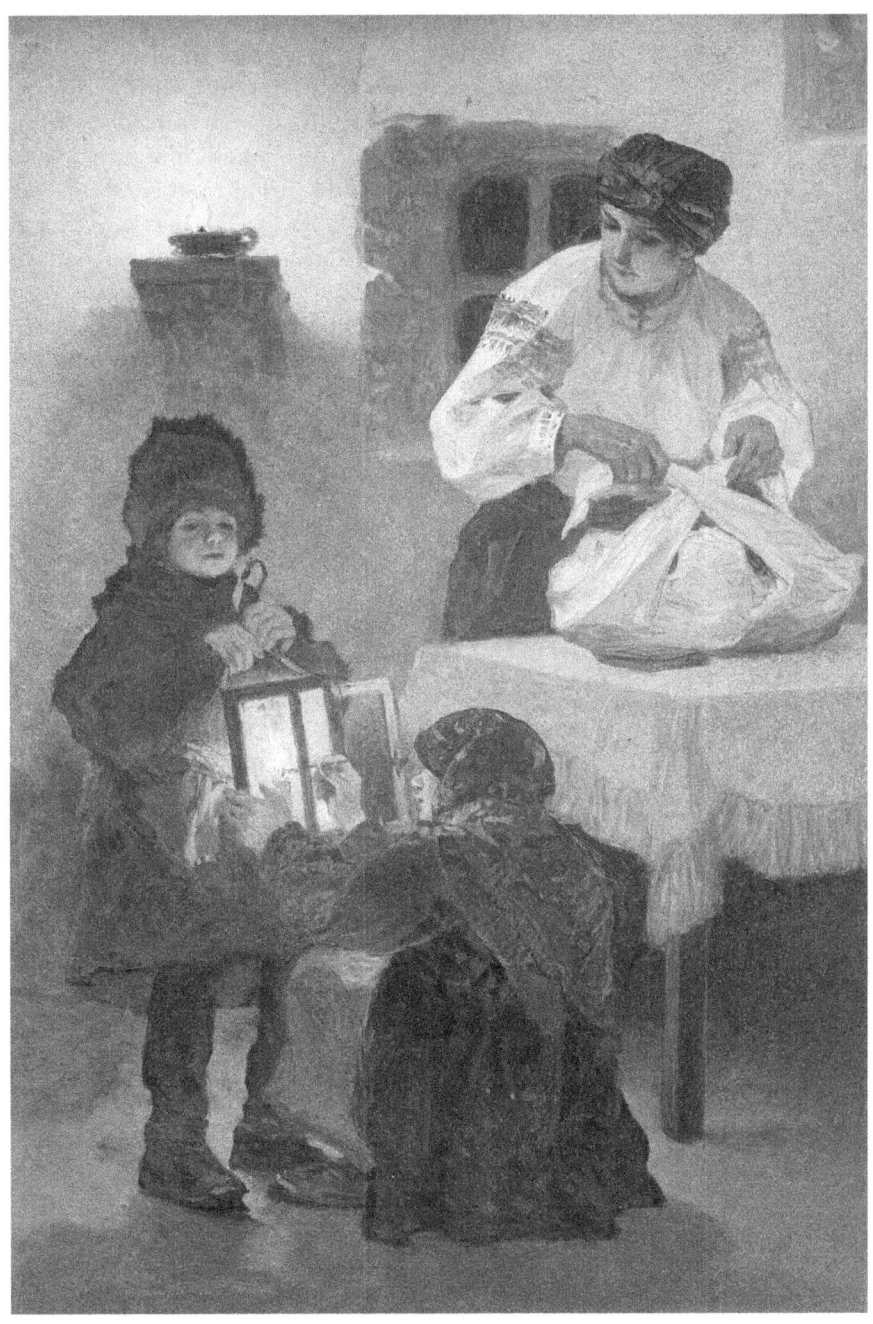

'In preparation for Easter Sunrise Service' by Ivan Yizhakevych (1902).

16. To give rushnyky – refers to an ancient Ukrainian custom of svatannia (making a marriage proposal). A young woman's suitor would send his representatives, called 'svaty' (plural; svat, singular) or 'starosty' (plural; starosta, singular), to her home to convey his marriage proposal. If the woman agreed to the proposal, she handed her rushnyky to the svaty (starosty) and her suitor. The custom differs in various regions of Ukraine.

(See illustration on page 66.)

17. One of the folk names for the second day of Easter celebrations is 'Oblyvanyi Ponedilok' [Pouring Monday]. See Yaroslav Pstrak's 'Oblyvanyi Ponedilok' on page 37.

one, for whom she will give a rushnyk[16] after *Hrobky Week*, and then after the Feast of the Ascension, they will hold their wedding during *Green Week*". In Podillia on the third day of the Bright Week the young men hire musicians and when lads invite girls to dance, the latter gift them with *pysanky*. In Tarasivka village, Kupyansk county, a groom must give a *pysanka* to his bride.

In Old Serbia on the second day of Easter celebrations, after the religious procession on the street, young wives (women who were wed during that current year) together with their mothers-in-law, approach men, presenting them with two red eggs each (Yastrebov 1886, p. 121).

According to a popular Czech belief, an exchange of *krashanky* strengthens friendship (Stranecka 1888, p. 10).

In Kyiv region and in Podillia on the second day of Easter celebrations, children go from house to house to greet with Easter. The mistresses of the houses that they visit already have their *krashanky* and *pysanky* waiting on top of the oven, whereas the *paska* [Ukrainian Easter bread] is on the table. If they are pleased with the children, they give eggs. However, if they are dissatisfied, then it is a slice of *paska* for the visitor (Maksymovych 1876–80, vol. 2, p. 471).

In Kyiv region and in *Galician Rus* [Halychyna or Galicia, Ukraine] on the second day of Easter celebrations,[17] at dawn, lads visit the houses where grown-up girls live, and if they catch them still sleeping or not ready, they pour water on them. Waiting for them, the girls put a couple of *krashanky* in a bucket in advance (Maksymovych 1876–80, vol. 2, p. 472). This custom exists from ancient times. In his *Description d'Ukranie* [Description of

Ukraine] Beauplan (1651) wrote: "In the morning of the next day after Easter, crowds of young men roam the streets, catch young women, take their captives to a well and pour about five or six buckets of water on them, so that the poor things have no dry spot left on them. This game is allowed only until noon. On Tuesday it is the turn of the girls, who take their revenge with great cunning. Having hidden in some house and prepared mugs with water, they put one girl on guard who, on seeing a young man, gives a sign. The other girls run out of the ambush and catch him, issuing terrible screams, which their friends from neighbouring houses run towards. Two or three strong girls hold the boy by the hands, while the rest souse him in water from the mugs."

This custom is also found outside Ukraine. The Czech call it 'pomlazka' and it involves young people, both men and women; first they 'hit' each other with willow twigs and then they present each other with *pysanka* or kraslitsa. Already the 14th century Czech literary monuments mention this practice, also referring to the use of *pysanky*. A church sermon, dated 1610, contains a detailed description of 'pomlazka' in Prague and explains that decorated twigs were sold on the streets; they were purchased by young men who then walked around with them on the streets and 'hit' women on their hands, 'demanding' *pysanky*. In Czechia, along with Easter 'pomlazka', a custom of pouring water on each other and gifting *pysanky* has also existed since the old days (Zibrt 1889, pp. 77–83).

Among the Poles there also were Easter customs of pouring water and gifting *pysanky*, and in some places they still remain. The custom of the Vitebsk Latvians is to pour water over and gift the eggs to shepherds on Saint George's Day, when they drive the cattle to pasture in the fields (Volters 1890, p. 3). There are similar customs among German and Slavic peoples (Afanasyev 1869, vol. 3, pp. 490–492).

Examining these spring customs, one can reach the conclusion that they are based on a symbolic depiction of nature in springtime, where the egg represents the sun, the water represents rain, and the ritual itself expresses a desire for fertility, and when concerning people, it is the wish for strength, health and joy.

The red egg gives health, strength and beauty. The villagers, on hearing the first spring thunder, wash their faces with the red egg[18] to acquire beauty, happiness and health. On Saint George's Day, when driving cattle into the field, they pat the horses with an Easter egg along their backs, from head to tail, chanting, "As the egg is smooth and round, you too, my horse, be pretty and full" (Afanasyev 1869, vol. 1, p. 538). In

18. 'To wash one's face
with red egg' – refers to
the ancient Ukrainian
ritual associated with
putting a red-dyed
egg, *krashanka*, into a
bucket with water and
then using that water to
wash one's face. As the
author writes, the people
believed that the red egg
would give them 'health,
strength and beauty'.

Kupyansk county, Kharkiv province, on Holy
Saturday they put two *krashanky* and a coin into
a bucket with water. Getting ready for the vigil
on Easter Sunday, either all members of the
family or just the young people will wash their
faces with this water for health and beauty.

The red egg also conveys fertility. During
Easter, peasants in Russia put a tub of wheat on
the table and bury an egg in it. These grains are
then kept for sowing. On their way to sow flax,
they put eggs in sacks with the grain, whereas
when sowing hemp they scatter eggshells in
the field. On Ascension Thursday they walk
on the fields sown with rye and throw red
eggs upwards so that the rye grows as tall as
the height of the thrown eggs (Afanasyev 1869,
vol. 1, p. 537). As for the Easter eggs in Lebedyn
county, Kharkiv province, here they keep a
couple of *krashanky* up until Saint George's
Day (23 April), on which day they go to the
rye fields, roll *krashanky* on the green shoots
and then bury them in the ground in the field,
for rye ears to be full and stand tall. During
the harvest they dig up the buried eggs. In
Czechia they bury Easter eggshells in the fields
(Stranecka 1888, p. 9).

Mykhaylo Maksymovych (1856)
observed that when a beekeeper (in Kyiv region)

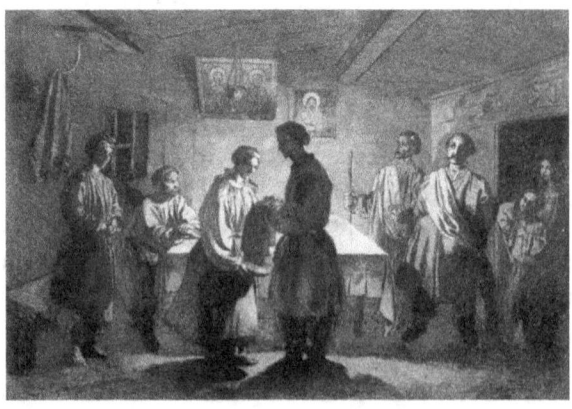

*'Starosty' by
Taras Shevchenko (1844).
See footnote 16 on page 64.*

goes to the apiary to greet his bees with Easter, he brings them a **'bezkonechnyk'** [eternity band] *pysanka*, which has one unbroken line drawn around it. He puts the *pysanka* under the first or corner beehive, which is called 'the master', and on which incense always lies, and on the main beehive, 'Zosym',[19] which is always placed in the middle of the apiary (Maksymovych 1876–80, vol. 2, p. 472). Exactly the same custom presently exists in Kupyansk county. In Katerynoslav province the eggshells from the blessed eggs are delivered to the bees in spring.

19. Zosym – is the name that Ukrainian beekeepers used to give their main beehive. 'Zosym' is a Ukrainian version of 'Zosimus', as in Saint Zosimus, patron of bees.

In Kupyansk county either *krashanky* or just their shells are used to protect the bread from the mice. Having brought new sheaves of wheat from the field they put four sheaves crossways, and underneath them they put the *krashanky* shells and the bones from a piglet cooked for the Easter occasion, and then they build a stack on top of it.

In Lebedyn county they put aside the first few *krashanky* and keep them in the house, as a means of preventing lightning strikes occurring over their courtyards. In Czechia, to protect a house from a lightning strike, they throw an egg that was laid on Maundy Thursday and then blessed on Easter over the house (Wanklova 1888, p. 7 & Afanasyev 1869, vol. 1, p. 538).

In Russia, if a fire occurs they take an egg that has been used to exchange Easter greetings on the first day of the Bright Week and carry it around the burning building, believing that the fire will not spread further. When thrown into the flames, this egg immediately extinguishes the fire (Afanasyev 1869, vol. 1, p. 538). In Kupyansk county, an Easter egg that was received in the church from a priest is kept as means of protection from fire. In the same county a belief is recorded that in the event

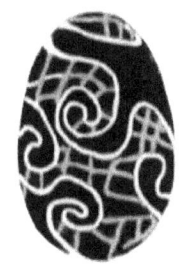

'Bezkinechna' [eternity band] pysanka (Kulzhynskyi 1899, table 6, no. 1).

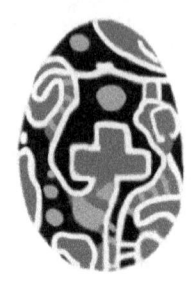

'Bezkonechnyk' [eternity band] pysanka (Kulzhynskyi 1899, table 5, no. 6).

of a fire, the first few eggs, which were dyed during the epitaphios procession, will help. In Neberdzhaievska village, Kuban region, the means of safety from fire is considered to be a *pysanka* that was received on the first day of the Easter holidays from the priest. In the case of fire, this *pysanka* is thrown into the direction from which the wind is blowing, to make it change its course. Exactly the same custom exists in Croatia.

Important medicinal properties are also attributed to Easter eggs. In Kalynove village, Kupyansk county, if someone is suffering from fever for a long period of time and nothing else helps, a *krashanka* that has been kept in the church at night on the eve of the Easter Sunday,is then hung on the neck of the patient. An identical belief is recorded in Kuban region. In Tenhinska village [Kuban region], in cases of fever patients, they either use the blessed *pysanka* eggshell to fumigate around the sick or hang the eggshell on their necks. The same custom is observed in Starokorsunska village.

In Lebedyn county and in Kuban region, *krashanky* are used to treat jaundice: they either dry several blessed *krashanky*, triturate the yolk and give it with water during jaundice; or they fumigate the jaundice patient using *krashanka* eggshells.

In Arapovka village, Kupyansk county, *krashanky* are used as a remedy for erysipelas.

Pysanky have important protective powers for guarding against the evil eye, as well as from witches harming cows or hens. In Kupyansk county and in Kuban the swollen udders are fumigated with *pysanka* eggshells. An especially characteristic use of *pysanka* shells and other remainders of the blessed Easter lunch as an amulet against witchcraft exists in Zelenchukska village, Kuban region. Having gathered leftovers (eggshells, breadcrumbs and so on) they drill a cow's horn and, after sprinkling it with holy water, they fill the hole. They do this to protect cows from the harm of witchcraft.

In Kupyansk county and in Kuban, they take *pysanky* to the cemetery and place them on graves or bury them in the ground. In Arapovka village [Kupyansk county] the following custom is observed: "At Easter they go to the cemetery and bury eggs. On the next day they dig them up and hand them out to children. If all *krashanky* are intact, then it means that the departed soul is pleasing to God. However, if someone else or if dogs have dug them up, then the soul is not pleasing to God and it is unknown how to help the soul." A belief exists that if you take the *krashanka* that you received first on Easter, and put it on the grave, then the dead can hear everything you say to them. In Starokorsunska village, on the first day of Easter, the senior member of the family brings to church some *pysanky* that have been cooked on Thursday and distributes them to commemorate the infants who died prior to being christened. Connected with this custom there is a ritual in Kupyansk county of throwing *pysanky* shells into the river for the *rusalky* and those who have drowned. According to folk beliefs, in ancient times people used to go to rivers to 'exchange Easter greetings' with *rusalky* and at the same time they distributed *krashanky* and *pysanky*, having rolled them in advance on the shore. The last detail brings us to a very popular 'kotok' [rolling] game [a folk game involving Easter eggs].

The earliest documentary evidence of the 'rolling' of eggs on Easter dates back to the 14th century, whereas the 'knocking' of the eggs goes back to the 17th century.

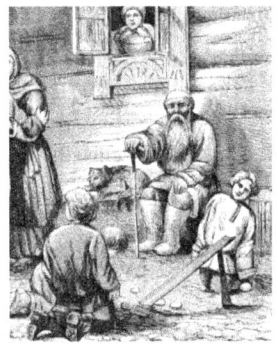

Detail of: 'Christ is risen!' Viktor Vasnetsov (1885).

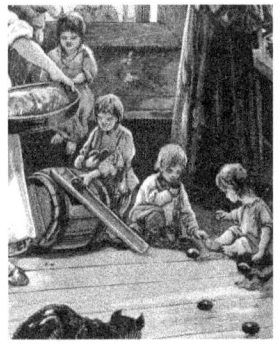

Detail of: 'Bright Easter Sunday in a village' by Nikolay Karazin (1885).

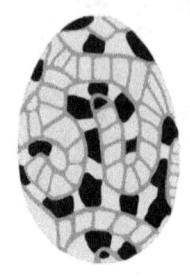

'Bezkonechnyk'
[eternity band] pysanka
(Kulzhynskyi 1899,
table 9, no. 8).

The Russian 17th century monastery mandates prohibit Easter games in 'bytky' [a folk game involving Easter eggs] (Afanasyev 1869, vol. 1, p. 537). If our opinion that the custom of 'rolling' eggs symbolically expresses the movement of the sun across the firmament of heaven is true, then it can be assumed that there is great antiquity behind these games. Nowadays this child's game remains popular in Russia. It is depicted in illustrations by N. Karazin (1885) and V. Vasnetsov in *Niva* (1885).

The number of local Ukrainian versions of the games with Easter eggs is insignificant.

In Kupyansk county, Kharkiv province, they differentiate two games with *krashanky*: 1) 'navbytky' and 2) 'navkotky'. The 'navbytky' is played as follows: a boy, having tapped his teeth firstly with the thinner and then with the thicker ends of the egg, selects 'a mark'. He holds his egg so that only the thinner end is visible, and the other boy knocks on it with the thinner end of his egg. Then they hit the eggs with their thicker ends. The winner is whoever's egg remains intact. The 'navkotky' is played like this: they roll the eggs in the small furrow, or sometimes simply from a mound, and whoever's rolling egg knocks aside or hits another's egg, wins (Ivanov 1889, p. 41). This game has not always been played completely honestly by the children: sometimes a few days before the holiday the children strengthen their eggs as follows: with an awl they pierce a hole in the eggshell, releasing the content of the egg and replacing it with wax, reinforcing the egg. They also make artificial eggs from dough and paint them with red dye.

An identical game of 'navbytky' is also noted in Poltava region (Sementovskyi 1843).

In Katerynoslav province they play the games of 'slipets' [blind man] and 'kytets' [roller]. The first game is played as follows:

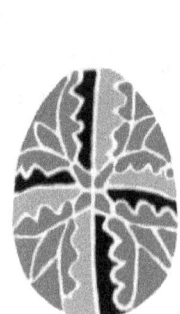

'Sorochi lapky' [magpie
feet] pysanka (Kulzhynskyi
1899, table 6, no. 8).

there are two participants. One puts an egg on the line, while the other participant makes at least a few steps back and tightly binds his eyes with a hat. Then he turns around once or several times (usually, the further the egg lies, the fewer turns he makes). For example, only one turn when further away, whereas in closer proximity the more turns are required (but no more than three), and then he walks towards the egg. If he walks in the right direction and stops near the egg, he wins. There are also two players in 'kytets'. One lays an egg on the line, while the other player, who walks away at the agreed distance, stands in a soldier's posture (heels together, toes apart), bends and puts his hand holding an egg to the ground, so that it is positioned just between the toes of his boots and then he quietly rolls the egg. If he hits the former egg, then he wins. 'Navbytky' happens to be a rarely played game.

In Kyiv province (Kaniv county) 'kotiuchka' – the rolling of the *pysanky* – takes place in the first two days of Easter [celebrations], whereas 'navbytky' are held in the first three days of Easter [celebrations] as well as during *Hrobky Week*. These games are almost identical with the Kharkiv 'navbytky' and 'navkotky' (Chubynskyi 1872–78 vol. 4, p. 43).

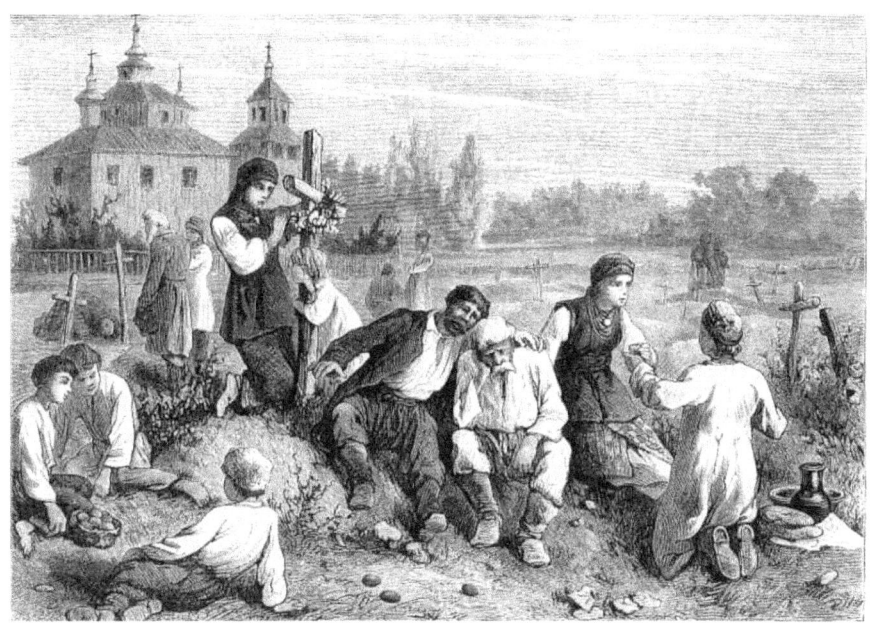

'Provody on Tomyna Sunday in Ukraine' by Kostiantyn Trutovskyi (1877)
[see definitions of 'Hrobky Week' and 'Tomyna Sunday'].

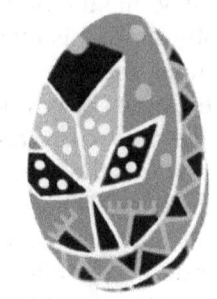

'Husiachi лapкy' [goose feet] pysanka (Kulzhynskyi 1899, table 8, no. 10).

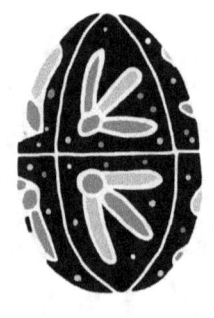

'Kuriachi лapкy' [hen feet], pysanka (Kulzhynskyi 1899, table 12, no. 1).

In Galicia [Halychyna] there is also a 'navbytky' game, which is called here 'proba pysanok' [test of *pysanky*]. Young men play using the *pysanky*, which they have received from girls (Lozynskyi 1859, p. 509).

In Kuban region children also play in 'navbytky' and 'katky' [also known as 'navkotky].

Games using *krashanky* are not limited to Bright Week and *Hrobky Week*. In many parts of Ukraine, after supper on Saint George's Day, girls go out into the fields sown with rye to roll their *krashanky* and then bury them in the ground until harvest (Maksymovych 1876–80, vol. 2, p. 485).

During Easter, the Poles in Plock province, both children and adults, play 'bytky' and 'katky', and these games are identical to the Ukrainian ones (Petrow 1878, p. 17).

The fact that 'kytets' game has a mythical and symbolic significance is evident by the custom of Latvians practising this game in spring, in honour of the solar deity, Usen. When the herdsmen drive horses out into the pastures overnight for the first time [after winter], the horse owners give them four or ten eggs per horse. The herdsmen make charcoal marks on the eggs and cook them. Sometimes they throw an egg into a thick willow bush for the horses to be handsome, or put the egg into an oak hollow for the horses to be strong. In Polish Livonia this custom usually takes place on the eve of Saint George's Day. The herdsmen knock on each other's eggs, and the one whose egg is strongest announces: "My horse is stronger." There is a song that invites people to bring a hundred eggs in sacrifice to Usen. Another song tells that Usen himself gifts eggs (Volters 1890, pp. 26–28).

Rolling *pysanky* as a symbol of the sun

corresponds to the rolling on a table of another sun symbol, a wedding wreath (for more details see my work *O Svadebnykh Obriadakh* [About wedding ceremonies] (Sumtsov 1881, pp. 79–89). There are some Ukrainian and Belarusian songs that mention how girls, having coiled a wreath, rolled it on the table (Metlynskyi 1854, p. 143 & Shein 1874, p. 361).

In some instances, the rolling of an object on the ground can represent the dedication, or rather the sacrifice, of the object to the sun. Apparently, such representation is depicted in the following market ritual, which is described in H. Kvitka-Osnovyanenko's *Soldatskyi Portret* [A Soldier's Portrait] (1833). A vendor, Yavdokha, came to the market with her palianytsi[20]: "The young women shout to Yavdokha: 'Come on, woman, choose a place for our sales to be successful. You are our head, where you set up, we will as well, near you.' Yavdokha took a palianytsia from someone else's box, stood facing east, crossed herself three times then rolled the palianytsia opposite the sun. The palianytsia fell near a soldier's portrait. The women, having mistaken the portrait for a live soldier, refused to set up near the soldier and so Yavdokha 'performed acts of witchcraft' with the second palianytsia." This peculiar witchcraft ritual suggests the cult of the sun.

Pysanky are rarely offered for sale. In Boromlia village, Okhtyrka county, I used to come across them at the markets during the last days of Holy Week. I bought a *pysanka* for five *kopiyky*, which was professionally made, whereas for ordinary ones I paid one *kopiyka* each. In *Ot Tobi i Skarb* [Here's a Treasure for You] (Kvitka-Osnovyanenko 1837), which was written in the early 1830s, a girl put aside one of the *pysanky* that she made, which was the best-

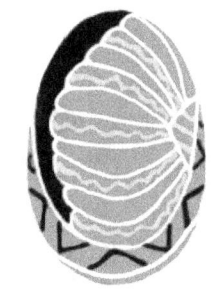

'Shuliachi lapy' [falcon feet] pysank (Kulzhynskyi 1899, table 7, no. 14).

20. Palianytsi (plural; palianytsia, singular) – are round loaves of bread.

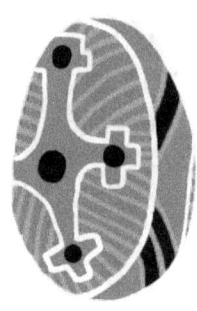

'Kryzhovyi khrest' [cross]
pysanka (Kulzhynskyi
1899, table 9, no. 14).

21. Horohvianyky (plural;
horohvianyk, singular) –
are pancakes made with
pea flour.

drawn one, for her fiancé, "... She will take the rest of them with her sisters tomorrow, on Holy Saturday, to the city, and, when they sell them, they will buy ribbons, paper for making doves, gold leaf and everything else they need; and whatever they do not sell, they can exchange during the holiday festivities for some nuts, pickled crab apples, horohvianyky[21] and all other sorts of goodies." *Pysanky* are also used as a payment for [a turn on] the swings nowadays in several parts of Ukraine, such as Kharkiv and Kuban regions.

In Volyn and Kuban and occasionally in Kharkiv region they hang *pysanky* under the icons, or under the icon lamps. In Temriuk town, they make holes at the opposite ends of a raw *pysanka*, and suck out the content of the egg with their mouths, then they pull through it a ribbon or thread and tie it to the icon lamp.

In Volyn they use *pysanka* eggshells, which as far as possible they try to preserve intact with the aid of wax, for making such fripperies as jugs, liqueur glasses and tiny vases (*Elisavetgradskiy Vesnik* [Elysavethrad Herald], 1889, no. 103).

Pysanky or their shells are stored for the whole year, until next Easter or until summer (Udziela 1888), or until the Ascension Thursday.

From the academic point of view, *pysanky* chiefly deserve attention and study for the sake of their ornaments. This ornamentation reflects their entire archaeological and aesthetic values.

We will divide the various forms of *pysanka* ornaments into the following categories of ornamentation: geometrical, solar, phytomorphic, zoomorphic, scevomorphic and religious. The solar ornamentation comes very close to the geometric and almost merges with it.

From the archaeological point of view, the most interesting fragments of the ancient past are presented by geometric and phytomorphic ornamentation.

The geometric and phytomorphic forms of ornamentation have existed since time immemorial. Monuments that were discovered in Santorini and Mykonos already contain highly developed phytomorphic patterns alongside the geometrical patterns.

The homeland of the geometric ornamentation is believed to be Hellas. However, a more plausible theory exists that Indo-European peoples brought the geometric style from the original Aryan homeland. The French scientist Jules Dumont d'Urville believes in the influence of Phoenician or in general even an Asian influence on the origin and development of the geometric style of ornamentation (Pavlutskyi 1889, pp. 61–64). The original forms of geometric ornamentation are so simple and unpretentious that they could have originated among various ancient peoples independently, and as such there is no need to search for the motherland of the geometric ornament. Of course, it is quite possible that over time the more advanced geometric pattern of one nation has influenced the ornamentation of other nations, and here one can emphasise the influence of the Asian

Geometric symbols

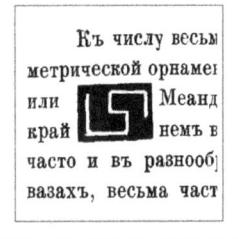

'Meander' ornament [1]
(Sumtsov 1891, p. 369).

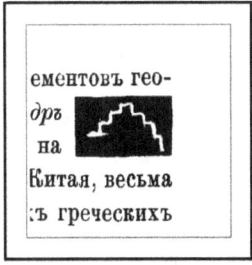

'Meander' ornament [2]
(Sumtsov 1891, p. 369).

East, where ancestral geometric ornamentation is distinguished by elegance and complexity. The extreme spread of the geometric style in all the countries along the shores of the Mediterranean Sea, as well as in Germany, Hungary, Denmark, Sweden, Russia, India and China, speak in favour of the opinion of the independent origin and, in some places, of the independent development. Fragments of vases with geometric patterns are also found in Jerusalem and Kuyunjik in Assyria (Pavlutskyi 1889, p. 62).

With few exceptions, when the geometric or phytomorphic figures are scattered all over the whole surface of the egg, the egg surface is usually divided by longitudinal or transverse lines, and sometimes by two longitudinal or two transverse lines, and sometimes by numerous longitudinal, or by four or even six transverse lines. These principal lines determine the form of the drawing. The transverse lines or strips in some places of Ukraine (for example, in Lebedyn county, Kharkiv province) are called **'poyasok'** [belt], and the *pysanka* itself is known as a **'poyasnytsia'** [with belt] or a **'bezpoyasnytsia'** [without a belt]. The main and transverse lines are sometimes joined by oblique and broken lines, which, as a result, at the intersections with longitudinal or transverse lines form triangles and **'rozeta'**[1] [rosette]. *Pysanky* no. 1 and no. 2 in Olha Kosach's *Ukrainskiy Narodnyi Ornament* [Ukrainian Folk Ornament] (Kosach 1876) can serve as examples of a pattern of intersecting longitudinal and oblique lines. Particularly beautiful is a complex line drawing on *pysanky* under the name **'sorok klyntsiv'** [forty wedges]. In fact, it does consist of forty wedges. These *pysanky* are found in Volyn, Podillia, Kharkiv regions and in Bulgaria. Sometimes *pysanky* with such patterns are called **'klyntsi'** [wedges] and contain only 24 wedges. When drawing straight and oblique lines on *pysanky*, the triangles become such a naturally flowing form of the ornament that we see no need to trace its succession from the archaic triangle, which is found on ancient bronzes, textiles and mosaics with symbolic meaning (Wankel 1888, p. 15). It should, however, be stipulated that a triangle on Moravian *pysanky* sometimes has independent significance in comparison with other geometric figures that are alongside it, such as the *pysanky* labelled nos. 20, 22 and 24 in Madlenka Wanklova's atlas (Wanklova 1888) (see page 84). Taking into account the limited availability of the information, we do not dare to completely eliminate the possibility of an archaic triangle being used in *pysanka* ornamentation.

The simple linear ornaments on *pysanky* include **'pletinka'** [Engl.,'network', also known as 'resheto' or 'syto', Engl., 'sieve'] (see page 77). This is one of the most ancient ornamentations, known since the era when mammoths inhabited Europe, and was depicted on the stone, as well as clay and bronze objects from the primitive era (Wankel 1888, p. 24). **'Pletinka'** [network] is often used on the Rhodes vases (such as oenochoai, hydriae and amphorae), which express the influence of Asian motifs in their ornamentation (Pavlutskyi 1889, p. 69). This pattern is found on the *pysanky* of the Slavic, Moravian (Wanklova 1888, nos. 4, 21, 43, 44 and 45) (see page 84 & page 85), Russian and Ukrainian peoples. We found the simplest and most archaic image of **'pletinka'** [network] on a Ukrainian *pysanka* from Chernihiv province. There is an identical pattern on a Moravian *pysanka* in Madlenka Wanklova's atlas, under no. 21 (Wanklova 1888) (see page 84). In my collection there is also **'pletinka'** [network] on a Russian *pysanka* from Shchigry county, Kursk province.

A dotted pattern is extremely common: on the ancient Greek vessels and other Greek objects from the banks of the Sea of Marmara and the Black Sea; on the silver and gold Scythian objects; in the ornamentation of all Slavs of more recent eras, especially Serbs and Czech-Moravians, which is located over their doors and windows, on walls and in embroideries; in Russia on the yokes and arcs; as well as among Czech-Moravians very often and in abundance on their *pysanky*. (See Madlenka Wanklova's atlas nos. 12, 13, 15, 17, 18, 20, 21, 24, 26 and 29, in a large number of dots nos. 31, 32, 34, 35 and 36, in conjunction with phytomorphic figures nos. 37–42) (Wanklova 1888) (see page 84 & page 85). The combinations of dots is very diverse: dots are positioned in a row one after the other, or stand in a triangle, or four dots make a square, or are attached by 'stalks' to lines, or surround leaves and flowers. The dotted pattern on Ukrainian *pysanky* has neither

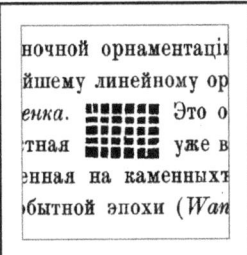

'Pletinka' ornament (Sumtsov 1891, p. 365).

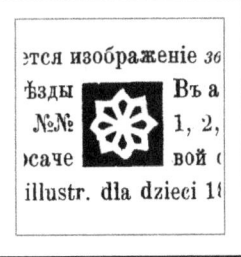

'Hretska zvizda' ornament (Sumtsov 1891, p. 367).

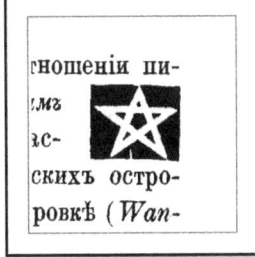

'Pentahrama' ornament (Sumtsov 1891, p. 368).

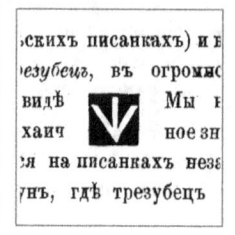

'Tryzub' ornament (Sumtsov 1891, p. 366).

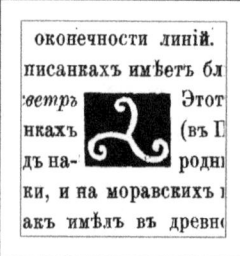

'Trykhvetr' ornament (Sumtsov 1891, p. 366).

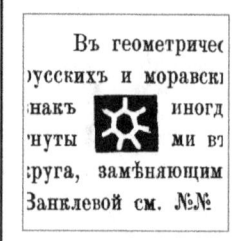

'Sontse' ornament (Sumtsov 1891, p. 367).

definite character nor important independent significance. Occasionally it is found on the **'poyasok'** [belt] of *pysanky* with crosses (in Kosach (1876) nos. 12 and 19) (see page 50), but more often it is positioned around leaves and flowers, where it completely transforms into the phytomorphic design. In some parts of Kamianets-Podilskyi province the *pysanky* with dotted patterns are known as **'kapanky'** (derived from 'kapaty' [to drip] with wax).

One can come across **'tryzub'** [trident] (see sidebar) occasionally on Ukrainian *pysanky* (in our collections it is on Kamianets-Podilskyi *pysanky*) and quite often on Moravian ones, which in the vast majority of cases is drawn without a handle. We are not inclined to assign an archaic meaning to this symbol, as we believe that it appeared on *pysanky*, regardless of the ancient scripts, such as runes, where the **'tryzub'** [trident] with its teeth positioned up symbolised a man or moon, whereas with its teeth positioned down, it symbolised the sky or cloud, and regardless of Phoenician and Greek writings, where the sign meant the letters 'm', 't' and 'psi' (Wankel 1888, p. 17). On *pysanky*, the **'tryzub'** [trident] appears at the end of lines, according to our assumption, as a natural result of drawing on eggs with a pin, when the remainder of the melted wax that was left on the tip of the pin is used on the ends of the lines.

The symbol **'tryskel'** [triskele] (or **'trykhvetr'** [triquetra]) (see page 78), which is similar to **'tryzub'** [trident] holds an independent position on *pysanky*. This symbol is found on Ukrainian *pysanky* (in Podillia) and in my collection it is noted under such folk names as **'ruta'** [rue], **'horikhovyi lyst'** [nut leaf] and **'pavuk'** [spider], as well as in Moravian *pysanky* – refer to Madlenka Wanklova's atlas under no. 26 (Wanklova 1888) (see page 84). In ancient times this sign had mystical and mythical significance, as a symbol of the movement of the sun across the firmament as well as a sign of fertility. The Phoenicians used **'trykhvetr'** [triquetra] as a symbol of Baal. In later times in Sicily this sign was used in heraldry. Often it is found in Denmark on ancient bronze knives and hatchets; on fibulae and other tumuli objects in Silesia, Hungary, Ukraine, Italy, Asia Minor and Syria (Wankel 1888, pp. 19–20). On some *pysanky* the **'trykhvetr'** [triquetra] (see page 78) acquires the appearance of a phytomorphic ornament.

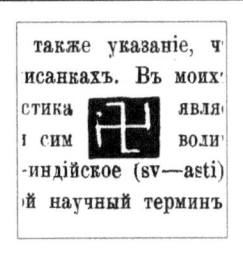

'Swastika' ornament (Sumtsov 1891, p. 369).

The geometric ornamentation on Ukrainian, Russian and Moravian *pysanky* often includes a symbol of **'sontse'** [sun] (see page 78); sometimes with a dot in the centre of the circle, sometimes with beams having curved ends and sometimes with dots around the circle, replacing the beams. See the Madlenka Wanklova's atlas *Moravské kraslice* [Moravian Easter eggs] under nos. 31, 33, 26, 47, 25, 26 (Wanklova 1888) (see page 84), and in Jindřich Wankel's article (Wankel 1888, p. 20) –

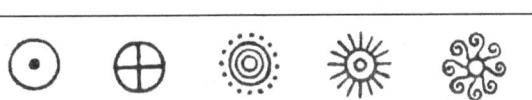

In my collections the symbol of **'sontse'** [sun] is found on one *pysanka* from Boromlia village, Okhtyrka county, on three *pysanky* from Kamianets-Podilskyi, on one from Volyn and on one from Kursk province (Russia). The Volyn *pysanka* consists entirely of these circles with beams; on other *pysanky* it is drawn in addition to other symbols. In general, this pattern on *pysanky* has a completely independent position, and, in all probability, in ancient times it symbolised the sun. Accepting this hypothesis, we naturally have to admit that the *pysanka* pattern with the symbol of **'sontse'** [sun] is the most ancient. According to

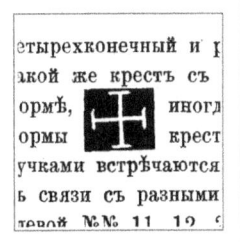

'Khrest' [cross] "with handles or bulges at the ends" as depicted on Moravian pysanky (Sumtsov 1891, p. 372).

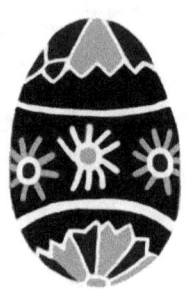

*'Zirka' [star] pysanka
(Kulzhynskyi 1899,
table 8, no. 9).*

two *pysanky* from our collection, from Podillia and Kursk, one can guess the setting in which the sun was positioned on the ancient *pysanky*. Both *pysanky*, and it is seen especially clearly on the Podillia one, have trees drawn and the signs of **'sontse'** [sun] are located on both their sides. The Podillia *pysanka* bears the appropriate name **'sosonka'** [diminutive form of 'sosna' (pine tree)]. The drawing represents the spring rebirth of nature under the sunbeams. This sign and its variants that symbolise the sun can be found on many prehistoric monuments: on bone, bronze and clay products, in the ancient Egyptian temples and pyramids, and on ancient Slavic embroidery.

A rather frequent image found on *pysanky* is one of a **'zvizda'** [or **'zirka'** – star], which is most often called **'hretska zvizda'** [Greek star]. In M. Wanklova's atlas such a star is found on *pysanky* under nos. 1, 2, 7, 8, 25 and 44 (Wanklova 1888) (see page 84 & page 85). In O. Kosach's *Ukrainskiy Narodnyi Ornament* [Ukrainian Folk Ornament] (Kosach 1876) see *pysanky* under nos. 3, 4, 10, 11, 12 and 13 (see page 50). In *Tygodnik Ilustrowany Dla Dzieci* 1889, no. 15, illustration under no. 25.

My collection includes about ten *pysanky* with the **'hretska zvizda'** [Greek star] motif (see page 77) on them, from Kharkiv, Poltava, Volyn and Kamianets-Podilskyi provinces. This is the most common and the most elegant form of a star. There are also other forms of stars, for example, with rays that have rounded tips. A rough drawing of this form of the star does not differ much from the phytomorphic ornament. The simplest and roughest shape of the star can be considered to be a quadrangular star, which is rarely found on the Ukrainian *pysanky*. *Pysanky* with stars are often found in Kuban and Poland as well. The stars are drawn most often on the wide longitudinal sides of the eggs, and

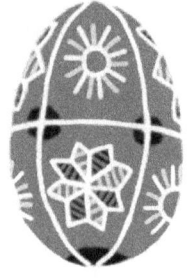

*'Zirky' [stars] pysanka
(Kulzhynskyi 1899,
table 8, no. 11).*

sometimes on the thin and thick ends. The rays diverge as in the **'hretska zvizda'** [Greek star], or converge to a central point.

From the archaeological point of view a lot of interest in the *pysanka* ornament is presented by **'pentahrama'** [pentagram] (see page 77). This mystical symbol is very widespread and goes back into deep antiquity. On the Caroline Islands people tattoo a pentagram on their skin (Wankel 1888, p. 21). The Sami people use the five-pointed star as a conventional reindeer brand and at the same time as an amulet (Kharuzin 1889). In Morocco, women hang pentagram charms on their children's necks. Antiochus I Soter in the campaign against the Gauls introduced this amulet to his troops. The bodyguards of the Byzantine emperors had pentagrams on their shields. It is also found on prehistoric swords, where, in all likelihood, it had the protective role of an amulet. In ancient times it was painted above the doors to protect the house from evil spirits and sorcerers. The pentagram had mysterious significance for the Pythagoreans and the ancient Hindus (Wankel 1888, p. 21). In the Hindu symbolism, Shiva is represented by a triangle oriented upright, like a pyramid, whereas Vishnu is represented by a triangle with the opposite orientation, with its tip downright, and when put one on top of the other, these triangles means a special sign, which serves as a symbol of fire and water, good and evil, and even a symbol of the universe (Nowosielski 1857, vol. 1, p. 185). Pentagrams are also found on Moravian *pysanky*, as with the *pysanka* under no. 32 in M. Wanklova's atlas (Wanklova 1888) (see page 85).

Some very characteristic archaic elements of geometric ornamentation also include the **'meandr'** [the 'meander' symbol] (see page 75). The meander is found in the ornamentation of the Far East, on the monuments of India and China, quite often and in a vast variety of combinations on ancient Greek vases, quite often on Etruscan vases, on many antiquities that were found in the Slavic countries as well as in modern times among the Slavs on their embroidery and pottery, and on Czech-Moravian *pysanky*. However, no meanders were found on the monuments of Iranian and Semitic peoples. Some scholars believe the home of meander to be in ancient Greece, others incline towards Etruria. Jindrich Wankel was of the opinion that this ornament has been known to the Slavs since ancient times (Wankel 1888). In all likelihood, various peoples at a certain stage of their spiritual development independently developed and fell in love with this form of ornamentation, which proved to be particularly useful for architecture and mosaics.

One scholar, who in the 1870s was engaged in the study of Ukrainian ornamentation and who collected for this purpose, among other things,

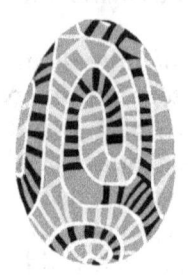

'Bezkinechna' [eternity band] pysanka (Kulzhynskyi 1899, table 6, no. 14).

pysanky, recently informed me that in his collection there were several *pysanky* decorated with **'svastyka'** [swastika] (see page 79). Recently, a Polish ethnographic journal, *Wisła*, also noted that the swastika is found on some Ukrainian *pysanky* (Zmigrodzki 1889). There are no such *pysanky* in my collections. The swastika is a primordial religious and mystical symbolic sign. The very word 'swastika' is derived from Sanskrit 'su-asti', and means 'good being' or 'to good health'. Another scientific term for this sign, which is less common, is 'tetraskel' (**'chotyrynih'** [four-legged]). Swastika is found on the ancient monuments of all the Indo-European nations. It was found among the Mongolians, Phoenicians, Etruscans, Finns and also the Americans. It gained popularity among the Gauls and Germans at the end of the Bronze Age, and among the Romans only in the 3rd century AD; however, it seems that the Etruscans used it for decoration. It is believed that the Asian Turanians borrowed the 'swastika' from the Aryans. In general, the swastika is a favourite religious symbol among the Aryans. A scientific hypothesis regarding the origin of the symbol exists, namely that the swastika was originally a tool for making fire, which was used in the sacred rituals, and later it began to signify the supreme deity of the sun, Apollo or Odin. Even nowadays light fascinates children. In ancient times light fascinated adults as well. To us, who reduce the darkness of the night with torches, lamps and electricity, it is difficult to imagine the horror experienced by prehistoric man, caused by the deep darkness that inhabited his imagination with monsters, and his joy when he saw the light or any of its symbols (Trachevskyi 1884, vol. 4, p. 14; Brinton 1889, p. 710; Zmigrodzki 1889, p. 970 & Wankel 1888, p. 18).

Several spiral lines, rings or whorls going around a *pysanka* constitute one of the most popular among Ukrainian *pysanka* ornaments, and are known as a **'bezkonechnyk'** [eternity band or never-ending line]: see *pysanka* under no. 21 in O. Kosach (1876) (see page 50). In my collections there are eight **'bezkonechnyk'** [eternity band] *pysanky* from Kharkiv, Volyn and Kamianets-Podilskyi provinces as well as from Kuban region. In its design an elegant **'bezkonechnyk'** [eternity band] *pysanka* from the town of Krasnokutsk, Bohodukhiv county [Kharkiv province], is exceedingly similar to a **'bezkonechnyk'** [eternity band] *pysanka* from Hulcha village, Ostroh county, Volyn province. The people bestow a mystical significance on *pysanky* with this ornament. During Easter, a beekeeper goes to greet his bees with Easter and brings them a **'bezkonechnyk'** [eternity band], under the first or expiatory beehive, which is called 'the master' the host, and on which there is always incense, (Maksymovych 1876–80, vol. 2, p. 472). The identical custom presently is practised in Kupyansk county, Kharkiv province: "Beekeepers place a **'bezkonechnyk'** [eternity band] *pysanka* under the beehive and then make sure it is well protected, in order for the bees to multiply for evermore. And this is the pure truth! It is called **'bezkonechna'** [eternal] because no matter how hard you look, you will find neither its beginning nor end: only some swirls and twirls." There are various forms of **'bezkonechnyk'** [eternity band]: coloured rings or spiral lines go across the egg or, occurring rarely, along the egg. I found *pysanky* of the latter kind in one record from Kamianets-Podilskyi province as well as in the collection of Fr Izmail Dmytriev from Lebedyn county, Kharkiv province.

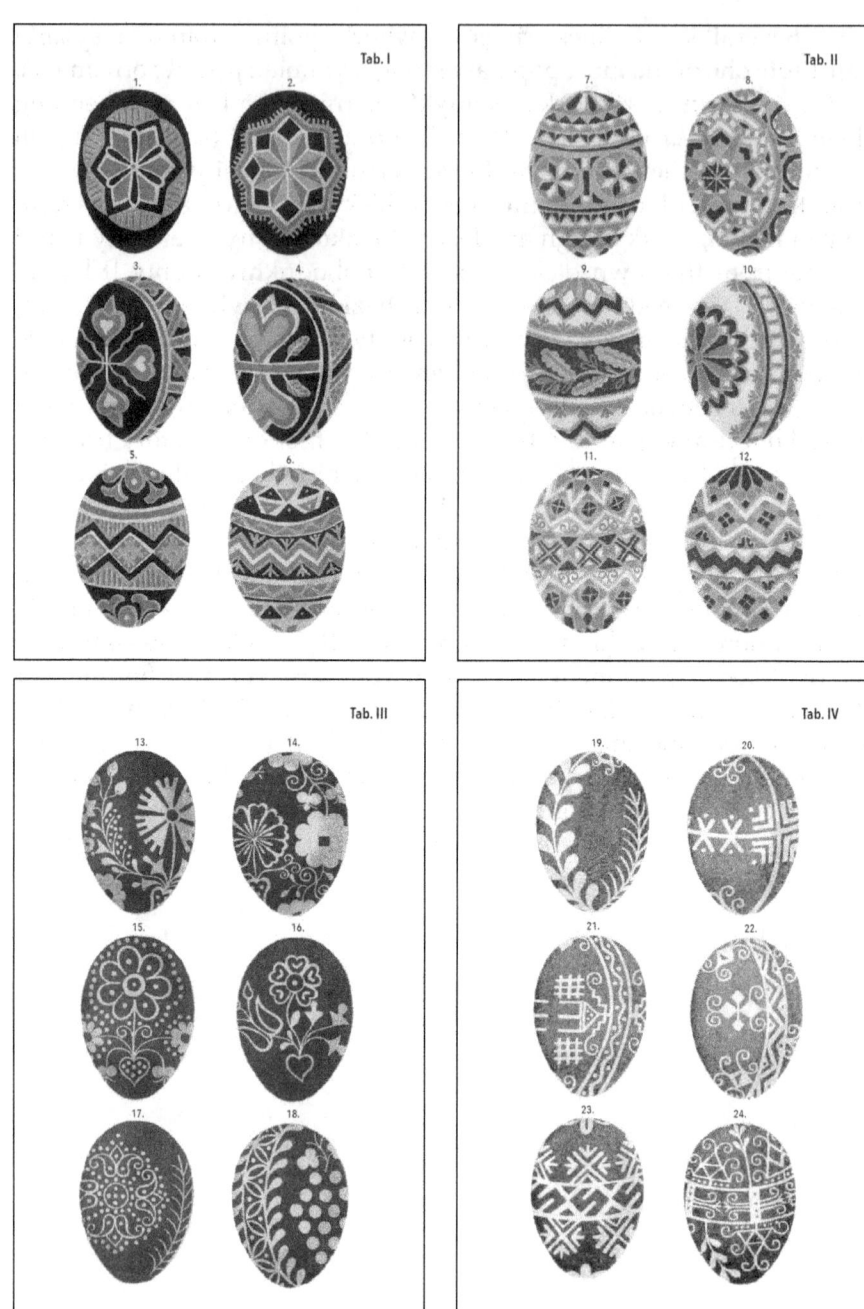

Pysanky nos. 1–24 in Madlenka Wanklova's atlas (Wanklova 1888).

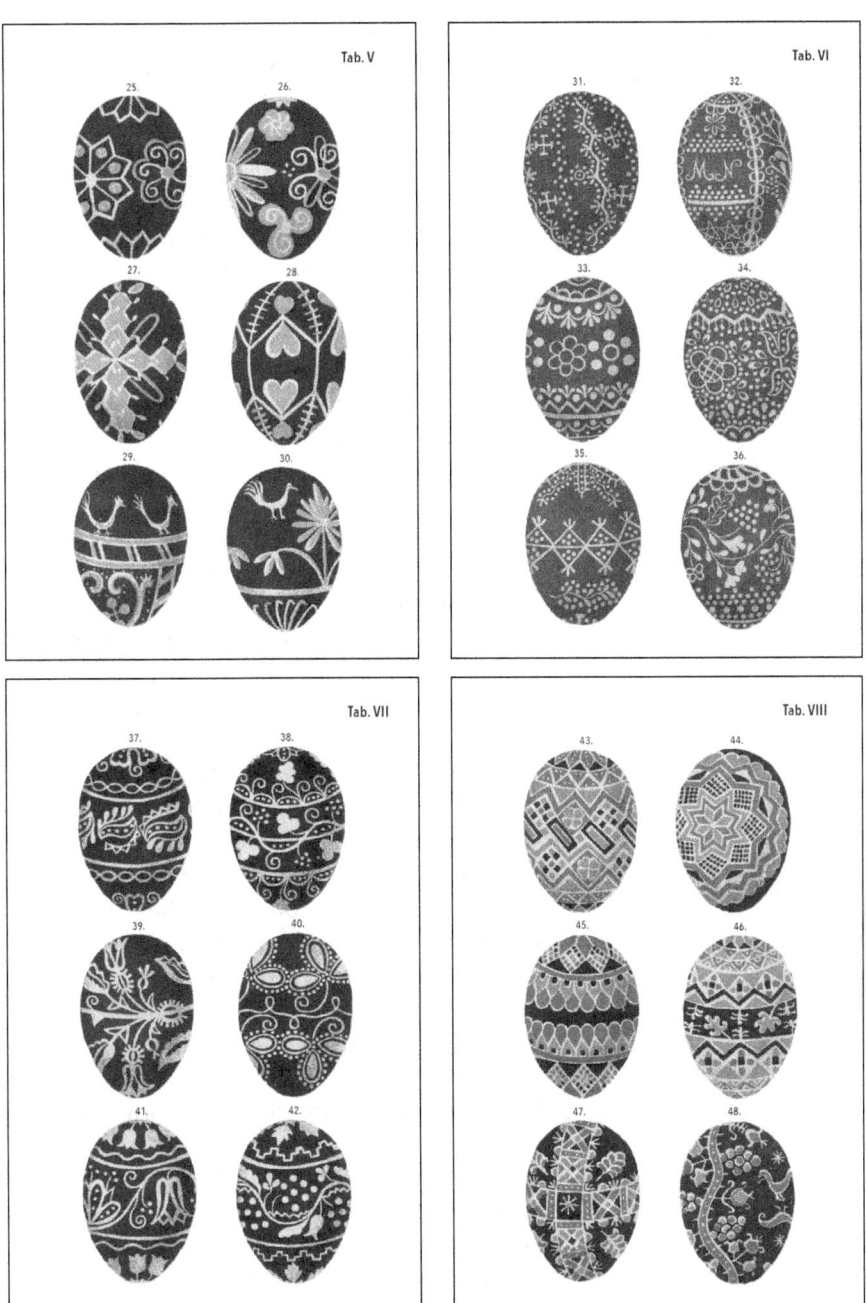

Pysanky nos. 25–48 in Madlenka Wanklova's atlas (Wanklova 1888).

Christian religious symbols

Christian religious motifs have little popularity in *pysanka* ornamentation, compared to other symbols. One can say that what is obscure in this regard nowadays, was perhaps also obscure and underdeveloped in the past. However, it does not speak against the folk's reverence for religiousness. This feeling has long been great. It was not in the power of a simple illiterate villager to introduce the Christian ornamentation to *pysanka*. With the arrival of educated artists in villages, as well as the spread of literacy among the villagers, inscriptions of a religious nature, images of the Saviour, Blessed Virgin Mary, the angels and a chalice were introduced to *pysanky*.

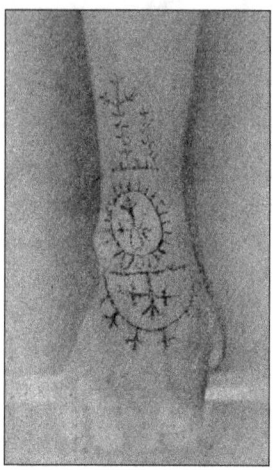

Tattooed crosses (Glik 1889, p. 83).

In some regions of Ukraine, for example in Kamianets-Podilskyi province, the religious tendency is captured in one of the most popular *pysanky* of the geometric style, **'sorok klyntsiv'** [forty wedges]. Such *pysanky* have come to mean either 'a forty-day Lent' or 'forty martyrs'. In some places the *pysanka* is drawn on the Feast Day of the Forty Martyrs [22 March]. There is a *pysanka* in my collection from Podillia province, which is called **'plashchanytsia'** [epitaphios] and depicts an equilateral four-armed cross with four peculiar coloured curls in the corners at the intersection of the cross's lines. In Ostroverhivka village, Kharkiv province, an experienced *pysanka*-maker, [Mrs] Holovchykha, among others, draws *pysanka* known as **'ikonostas'** [iconostasis]. In Galicia [Halychyna] there are the following *pysanky*: **'tserkovka'** [diminutive form of 'tserkov' or 'tserkva' (church)], **'dzvin'** [bell or ring] and **'popovi ryzy'** [priest's vestments] (*Tygodnik Ilustrowany Dla Dzieci* 1889, no. 15).

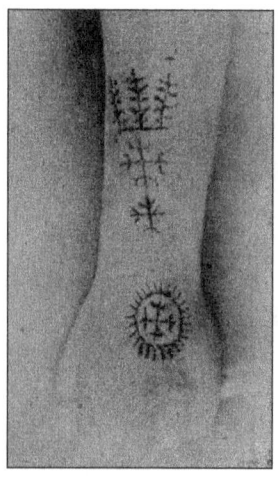

Tattooed crosses (Glik 1889, p. 83).

'Khrest' [cross] *pysanky* are very common. It is known that long before the emergence of Christianity the cross held a prominent position in ornamentation and, apparently, in symbolism. The cross has already become a customary ornamental detail on clay vessels found on the islands of the Aegean Sea, which archaeologists trace as far back as the 10th century BC (Pavlutskyi 1889, p. 60). However, there is no reason to assign the *pysanky's* crosses to pre-Christian times. Undoubtedly, we are dealing here with Christian ornamentation, which is easily available to the folk due to the simplicity of its design. Forms of crosses on *pysanky* are quite versatile. The most common is an ordinary 'Greek cross', which is four-armed and equilateral. Moravian *pysanky* depict an identical cross but with handles or bulges at the ends. Sometimes it can be a Saint Andrew's cross, shaped like the letter 'X'. These forms of the cross, mainly a simple Greek one and the one with handles on it, are found on the Ukrainian

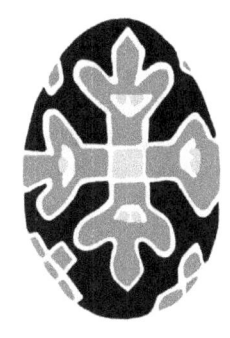

'Khrest' [cross] pysanka (Kulzhynskyi 1899, table 12, no. 10).

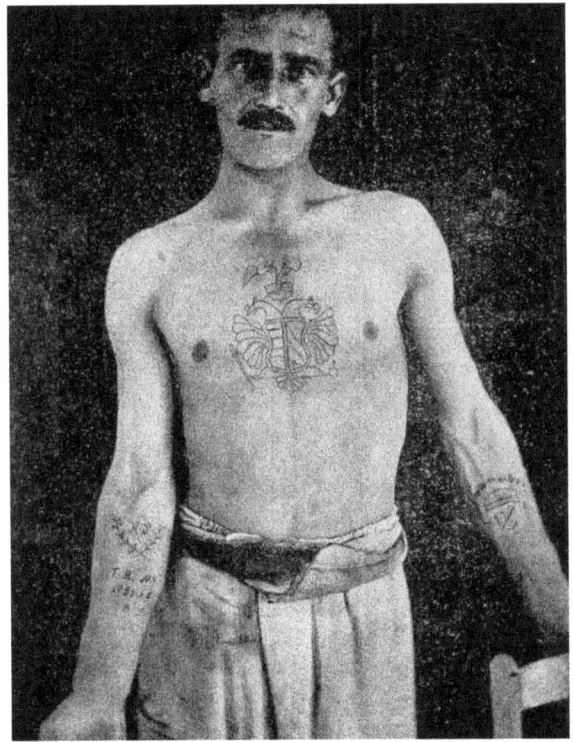

Tattooed crosses (Glik 1889, p. 84).

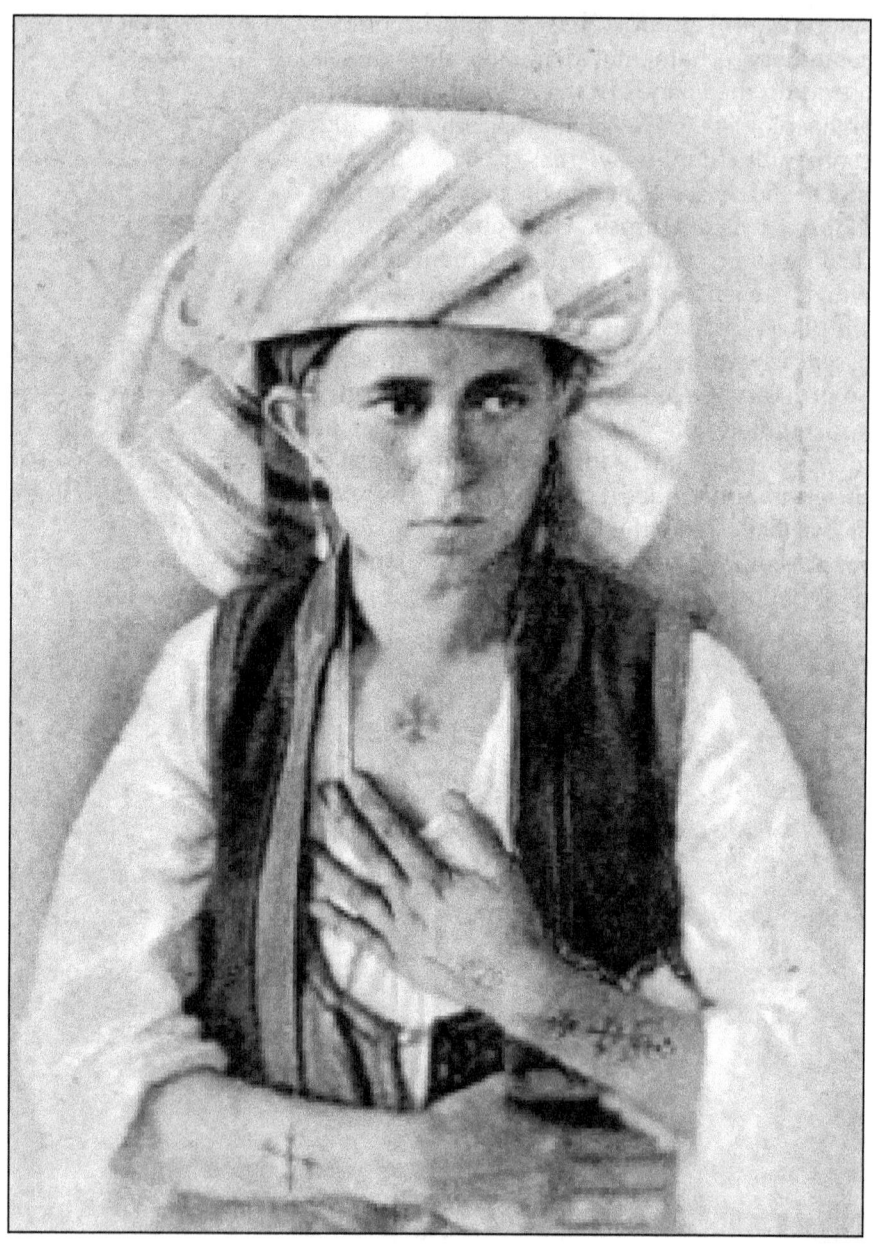

Tattooed crosses (Glik 1889, p. 88).

and Moravian *pysanky* due to the various elements of the geometric style (see *pysanky* nos. 11, 12, 20 and 23 (Wanklova 1888) (see page 84) and nos. 14 and 20 (Kosach 1876) (see page 50). All these forms of the cross were quite common in the Byzantine East. Usually, the Orthodox churches were, and continue to be built, in the form of a Greek cross. Such a cross was also often painted on the robes of Saints. The Greek cross with handles was introduced into the ornamentation of the temple of Saint Sophia in Constantinople. Currently, Serbian Catholics in Bosnia tattoo crosses with bulges at the ends on their arms (Glik 1889) (see page 88). As for the Latin cross with its elongated lower end, in the form of which most of the churches of Romanesque and Gothic styles are built in the Catholic West, we found only one in the collection of *pysanky* from Balakliya village, Zmiiv county, Kharkiv province. The presence of Saint Andrew's and Greek crosses on the Ukrainian and Czech-Moravian *pysanky* speaks in favour of an assumption of the Byzantine origin of *pysanka* ornamentation among the Slavic peoples.

O. Kosach's atlas (1876) contains some peculiar **'khrest'** [cross] *pysanky*: no. 14 (eight-armed cross), no. 19 (four-armed cross from flowers) and no. 20 (two small equilateral four-armed crosses, where one is inserted into the other) (see page 50). In my collections there are a few roughly executed crosses from flowers and a pretty elegant drawing of a cross laid on a star. Moravian **'khrest'** [cross] *pysanky* in M. Wanklova's atlas are: under no. 3 (see page 84) (which is similar to the Ukrainian *pysanka* in O. Kosach's atlas under no. 19 (1876), under no. 27 (an excellent drawing of a four-armed red cross from quadrangles on a black background and under no. 47 (a red cross that consists of many small crosses on a black background) (see page 50).

Geometric and phytomorphic ornaments on *pysanky* from Temriuk town, Kuban region, would definitely include a small **'khrest'** [cross]. This **'khrest'** [cross] is found on *pysanky* with **'sorok visim klyntsiv'** [forty-eight wedges], **'bezkonechnyk'** [eternity band], **'povna rozha'** [full mallow] and others.

In various places of Ukraine: in Kharkiv province, in Kamianets-Podilskyi as well as in Kuban region occasionally one can come across professionally made *pysanky* with images of the Saviour, Saint Mary or angels, with the inscription "Christ is risen", and with an image of a chalice or a heart pierced by an arrow.

Phytomorphic symbols

The phytomorphic ornamentation is found on many *pysanky*. In its popularity and artistry it is as good as a geometrical ornamentation. They draw either a whole plant, or, due to the small surface of the egg, parts of the plant: leaves and flowers on their own, or flowers on stems with leaves. The phytomorphic ornamentation often defines the name of *pysanka*: **'rozhevka'** [derived from **'rozha'** – mallow], **'khrinovyi lyst'** [horseradish leaf], **'sosna'** [pine] and so on. When a *pysanka's* phytomorphic ornamentation is complex then sometimes it acquires a complicated descriptive terminology. The most typical examples are the *pysanky* from Lebedyn county, Kharkiv province, which were kindly supplied to me by Fr Izmail Dmytriev, together with a well-constructed explanatory note. This collection consists of nineteen *pysanky* that are designed according to a strict system based on three foundations: **'vyshnevyi lyst'** [cherry leaf], **'dubovyi lyst'** [oak leaf] and **'rozha'** [mallow], where the difference in the pattern is determined by [1] the position of the leaves, that is, the end of the egg (rounded or pointy) on which the leaves are drawn, [2] whether the form of the leaf is large or small, and, finally, [3] whether a transverse line, **'poyasok'** [belt], is included, or not. Such ornamentation defines most *pysanka* terminology, for example:

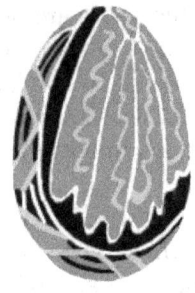

'Sosonka' [diminutive form of 'sosna' (pine tree)] pysanka (Kulzhynskyi 1899, table 7, no. 15).

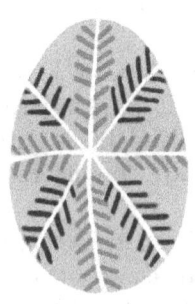

'Sosonka dribnesenka, kotra v poli v khlibi roste' [a tiny pine tree that is growing in a wheat field] pysanka (Kulzhynskyi 1899, table 8, no. 2).

Pysanka **'vyshnevyi lyst'** [cherry leaf] can be:
1. **'Vyshnevyi lyst'** – **'bezpoyasnytsia'** [without a belt i.e. a transverse line is not included in the design].
2. **'Vyshnevyi lyst'** – 8 leaves are drawn.
3. **'Vyshnevyi lyst'** – 4 leaves are drawn on yellow background.
4. **'Vyshnevyi lyst'** – 4 leaves are drawn on white background.

Pysanka **'dubovyi lyst'** [oak leaf] can be:
1. **'Dubovyi lyst'** – 8 leaves are drawn.

2. **'Dubovyi lyst'** – **'bezpoyasnytsia'** [without a belt i.e. a transverse line is not included in the design].

3. **'Dubovyi lyst'** – **'bezpoyasnytsia'** [without a belt]; 4 leaves are drawn.

4. **'Dubovyi lyst'** – **'bezpoyasnytsia'** [without a belt]; 4 leaves and acorns are drawn.

5. **'Dubovyi lyst'** – 2 leaves are drawn.

6. **'Dubovyi lyst'** – the side longitudinal line; 2 leaves are drawn.

7. **'Dubovyi lyst'** – the side transverse line; 2 leaves are drawn.

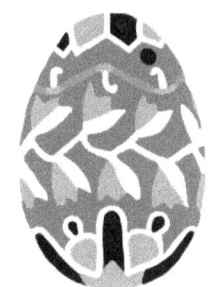

'Khmelyk' [hop] pysanka (Kulzhynskyi 1899, table 6, no. 6).

Pysanka **'rozhevka'** [derived from 'rozha' – mallow] can be:

1. **'Rozhevka'** – 6 flowers are drawn.

2. **'Rozhevka'** – 4 **'rozha'** [mallow] (half-a-flower) symbols are drawn.

3. **'Rozhevka'** – 2 **'rozha'** [mallow] (half-a-flower) symbols are drawn.

4. **'Rozhevka'** – 2 **'rozha'** [mallow] (not a full flower, known as **'sheludivka'**) symbols are drawn.

5. **'Rozhevka'** – 2 **'rozha'** [mallow] (full flower) symbols are drawn on the ends of an egg.

6. **'Rozhevka'** – 2 **'rozha'** [mallow] (not a full flower, known as **'sheludivka'**) symbols are drawn on the ends of an egg.

7. **'Rozhevka'** – 2 **'rozha'** [mallow] (not a full flower, known as **'sheludivka'**) symbols are drawn on the sides of an egg.

8. **'Rozhevka'** – 4 petals are drawn on yellow background.

The explanation of this terminology needs to include clarification of "5) **'rozhevka'** – two **'rozha'** [mallow] (full flower) symbols are drawn on the ends of an egg". It means that the two symbols of **'rozha'** [mallow] are drawn on the top and bottom ends of an egg with their petals coming down to the middle of the egg, if there is no **'poyasok'** [belt]; otherwise, if there

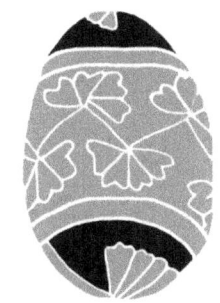

'Khmelyk' [hop] pysanka (Kulzhynskyi 1899, table 7, no. 9).

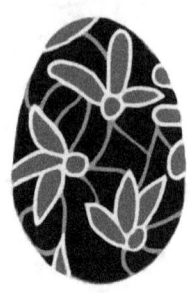

'Barvinok' [periwinkle] pysanka (Kulzhynskyi 1899, table 5, no. 1).

22. This complex terminology is observed only in Anyno village, Lebedyn county. In other places *pysanky's* names generally consist of one word (such as **'sakva'** [sack], **'sosna'** [pine] and **'khrestata'** [with crosses]), occasionally of two words (**'baraniachi rohy'** [ram horns] or **'kuriachi lapy'** [hen feet]), depending on the ornament. (Note from the author.)

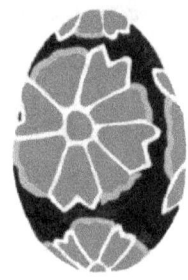

'Roza' [rose] pysanka (Kulzhynskyi 1899, table 7, no. 12).

is **'poyasok'** [belt], then the **'rozha'** [mallow] symbols, which are drawn on the egg's ends, are of a smaller size, and that is why such *pysanka* is called **'sheludivka'**; that is, it depicts a flower that is not full [incomplete] flower. When **'rozha'** [mallow] symbols are drawn on the wide sides of *pysanka*, then we have a 'side' *pysanka*.[22] *Pysanka* **'bokova rozha** [side mallow] **sheludivka'** is also found in Temriuk town, Kuban region.

'Vyshnevyi lyst' [cherry leaf], **'dubovyi lyst'** [oak leaf] and **'roza'** [rose] (the same [symbol] as **'rozha'** – mallow) are found on *pysanky* in Galicia [Halychyna], Katerynoslav province, Kuban region and in other areas with a Ukrainian population. [The symbol] **'roza'** [rose] is more common than other flowers.

In H. Kvitka-Osnovyanenko's novel *Ot Tobi i Skarb* [Here's a Treasure for You] (1837), there is "a coffee (in colour) **'rozha'** [mallow] was barely fitted on the whole egg and only a tiny leaf hardly found a place at the very end." The form of leaves is so often indistinct that it is difficult to determine the nature of the plant. There is a *pysanka* in my collection called **'poliova rozha'** [field mallow] from Ostroverhivka village, Kharkiv county, the drawing on which resembles a *pysanka* with **'dubovyi lyst'** [oak leaf] from Lebedyn county.

Pysanka with two symbols of **'rozha'** [mallow] (not a full flower, known as **'sheludivka'**), which are drawn on the ends of an egg, from Lebedyn county is similar to *Galician Rus* [Halychyna or Galicia, Ukraine] *pysanka* called **'podluzhna rozha'** (*Tygodnik Ilustrowany Dla Dzieci* 1889, no. 15, under no. 26). There is a *pysanka* known in Kamianets-Podilskyi province, which is called **'rozha z hrebintsiamy'** [mallow with combs or crests] (a flower is located in the middle of an egg and four lines ending with **'hrebinets'** [diminutive form of 'hrebin' (comb)] symbols divide it crosswise). In Kuban region there is a 'perevyta rozha' [intertwined mallow] with flowers on the longitudinal lines.

Among the rest of the plants, the plant that is most often depicted on *pysanky* is a pine. It is likely that this symbol ['sosna' – pine] is very ancient, because in most cases it is depicted in connection with the sun circles, which together supposedly represent the resurgence of nature in spring. 'Sosna' [pine] *pysanky* can be very beautiful, as one can see from the Volyn *pysanka* in my collection. 'Sosna' [pine] *pysanky* are known in Kursk province, Kuban and Galicia [Halychyna]. Galicians distinguish *pysanky* as 'velyka sosna' [large pine] (one branch along the whole egg) and 'mala sosna' [small pine] (four branches crosswise).

'Kosychata rozha' [*means asymmetrical and horizontal mallow*] *pysanka (Kulzhynskyi 1899, table 13, no. 8).*

We came across the following symbols of Ukrainian flora on *pysanky*: 'kozodrys' (Polish 'kosodrzew' or 'kosowka', *Pinus mughus* [mountain pine]), 'hvozdyka' [carnation], 'fialka' [viola], 'vynohrad' [grapevine], 'slyvy' (fruits) [plums], 'ruta' [rue], 'barvinkovyi lyst' [periwinkle leaf], 'popova mud' (flowers) [spindle flower] and 'horikhovyi lyst' [nut leaf]. These phytomorphic symbols adorn the *pysanky* from Kamianets-Podilskyi province. 'Hvozdyka' [carnation] is found on Kharkiv and *Galician Rus* [Halychyna or Galicia, Ukraine] *pysanky*. In Kamianets-Podilskyi province they also draw 'polunyshnytsia' *pysanka*, [derived from the word 'polunytsia' – strawberry]. In Anyno village, Lebedyn county, there is also *pysanka* known as 'khrinovyi lyst' [horseradish leaf], which is of a quite original design (combination of the coloured parallel stripes).

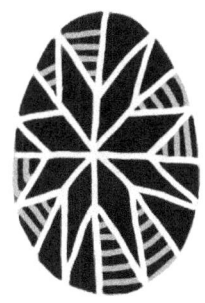

'Zelena rozha' [*green mallow*] *pysanka (Kulzhynskyi 1899, table 5, no. 15).*

In Temriuk town [Kuban region] one type of *pysanka* bears the name of 'ohirky' [cucumbers].

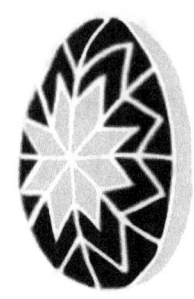

'Rozha' [malva] pysanka (Kulzhynskyi 1899, table 8, no. 15).

Some Polish *pysanky* depict 'palms' or 'pine branches' (Udziela 1888, p. 9). Various *pysanka* ornaments are achieved by a combination of 'stars' and 'pines'. There are also *pysanky* embellished with 'brooms' or 'poppies', which is a very elegant *pysanka*, where small poppy leaves, which are in the white colour of the eggshell, are carved on the blue background, (Wisła, 1890, vol. 3).

The atlas of Moravian *pysanky* includes very elegant drawings of leaves, flowers and flower-bells (Wanklova 1888, nos. 3, 4, 13–18, 26, 28, 30, 36, 38–42, 47 and 48) (here, see page 84 & page 85). Unfortunately, the atlas contains no information regarding the origin or the names of the plants depicted on the *pysanky*. The best *pysanky* presented from the artistic point of view are numbered 39–42 (leaves and bells in a spiral form encircling the entire egg).

Images of hyacinths, tulips and apples are found on Serbian *pysanky* (Svitlic 1889, p. 60).

Finding the zoomorphic ornament on *pysanky* is a rare occasion. The age of this style cannot be determined precisely. Some forms of zoomorphic ornamentation date back to ancient times, for example, the image of **'piven'** [rooster]. Others (such as **'rak'** [crayfish] or **'kuriachi lapy'** [hen feet]) can be viewed as the fortuitous result of one's imagination, which relies on the conditions of the people's contemporary everyday life. However, if we turn our attention to the ancient zoomorphic ornamentation in general, then, without going into details, it is sufficient to note that the drawings and carvings of animal figures constituted a part of the activities of the ancient cave dwellers of Europe and were performed so artistically that some researchers believed these drawings on stone, bone and bronze to be a modern forgery. The art of colouring originated during ancient times. Primitive people painted their bodies with charcoal, red clay, and red and yellow ochre. They also could have used the same paints to colour carved figures or eggs. Travellers who visited Australia, on having inspected the caves there, were amazed by the art, with frescoes portraying kangaroos, emus and dancing natives made on the cave walls (Tylor 1881, p. 300).

The zoomorphic ornamentation of *pysanky* occasionally depicts the whole animal. For the most part, they present only some of its parts (horns, feet and so on), which is justified by the small size of the material used.

The most widespread and, apparently, the oldest zoomorphic figure used on the *pysanka* is a bird, which most frequently is depicted in the form of a **'piven'** [rooster]. In H. Kvitka-Osnovyanenko's novel *Ot Tobi i Skarb* [Here's a Treasure for You] (1837): "Oryshka drew cherry-colour kissing birds and across the whole egg she wrote words that the deacon

Zoomorphic symbols

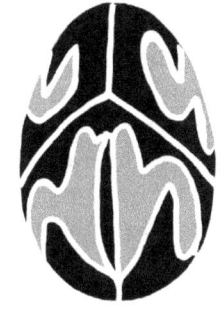

'Baraniachi rohy' [ram horns] pysanka (Kulzhynskyi 1899, table 10, no. 12).

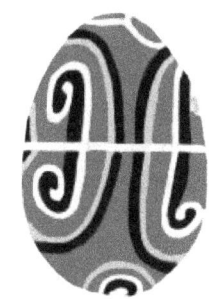

'Baraniachi rohy' [ram horns] pysanka (Kulzhynskyi 1899, table 9, no. 9).

Symeyon had composed and written down on a piece of paper:
Christ will be resurrected,
Let us kiss, my heart.

Oryshka was copying from that piece of paper, but being illiterate, she began with the wrong hand; and even those who are literate will understand nothing and will be unable to say whether it was a wording or a doodle." (Kvitka-Osnovyanenko 1837). A similar custom still exists in Kharkiv province. In Kupyansk county painters and artists draw kissing doves on *pysanky*. However, this form of zoomorphic ornament does not have the character of antiquity, and instead of the seriousness of intent that is typical to antiquity, it exhibits erotic and sentimental origins.

The **'piven'** [rooster] on a Russian *pysanka* in my collections and on three Moravian *pysanky* in M. Wanklova's (1888) atlas (nos. 29, 30 and 48) appears to be far more ancient (see page 85). Here, the **'piven'** [rooster] symbols are surrounded by trees and flowers, and on *pysanka* no. 48 there are also some added celestial symbols in the form of stars (see page 85).

Images of roosters and doves are found on the Serbian *pysanky* (Svitlic 1889, p. 62). I was also brought a picture of a *pysanka* from Bulgaria, on one side of which a large bird in a standing position was depicted; on the other side, the bird was in flight. It was difficult to determine the bird species.

On *pysanky* the **'piven'** [rooster] is a zoomorphic symbol of the sun, as evidenced by the undoubted sun symbolism of a rooster in many beliefs, proverbs, tales and rituals. As the herald of the dawn, the rooster became a symbolic signifier of the sun during ancient times. The riddle 'a rooster sits on a willow and lets its braids dangle down to the ground' is about the sun and its rays. Throughout Europe, the voice of the rooster is attributed with a mighty power – the demons, 'mertsi' [undead] and *upyri* [blood-sucking creatures] disappear at the first crow of a rooster. The wooden images of a rooster on the roofs in some areas of Germany and Russia serve as a protective talisman (Afanasyev 1869, vol. 1, p. 518).

There is a *pysanka* in my collection from Kamianets-Podilskyi province (supplied by Fr Rodkevych) called **'bdzhola'** [bee]; however, it is hard to guess from the drawing that it is a bee. The body is, in fact, bee-like – long and with yellow transverse stripes; the head, which is in the form of a crossbar, is of the same style; but instead of wings and in front of the head there are large red triangles. Priest Rodkevych expressed a supposition that the **'bdzhola'** [bee] *pysanka* might refer to 17 March, the feast day of Saint Alexius, who, according to the local folk beliefs, is a patron of beekeeping.

The same collection contains another rare *pysanka* – 'rak' [crayfish]. In this case there is no way one could guess the 'rak' [crayfish] from the drawing. The figure bears a strong resemblance to 'bezkonechnyk' [eternity band]: a spiral line circles the whole wide part of the egg facing the viewer, and a small cross-shaped figure is positioned in the middle of the line.

The same collection contains *pysanka* 'pavuky' [spiders' pattern], which without knowing its name can be mistaken for a *pysanka* with a phytomorphic pattern. There is no similarity to spiders: the 'poyasok' [belt] divides the *pysanka* into two longitudinal halves; a cross-like flower divides each half of the *pysanka* into four parts, and each of these parts contains three lines that are curved into a circle and sit on one stalk.

The same, Kamianets-Podilskyi, collection contains a *pysanka* entitled 'sharpanska mukha' [sharpan fly], which somewhat resembles a large fly: a belly with a long head, two wings at the belly and two long wings on each side. The *pysanka*-maker produced a flawed image, depicting two wings next to and of the same size as the head that is why the fly appears to be three-headed.

Occasionally, an image of a snail is found on the *Galician Rus* [Halychyna or Galicia, Ukraine] *pysanky* and, as such, these *pysanky* are called 'ravlyk' [snail] (Udziela, *Tygodnik Ilustrowany Dla Dzieci*, 1889, no. 15).

In the same *Galician Rus* [Halychyna or Galicia, Ukraine] area (namely, in Pokuttia) there is a *pysanka* with a winding line on the egg. This *pysanka* is called 'vuzh' [grass snake] (ibid).

A collection of *pysanky* that belonged to the former South-Western Division of the Russian Imperial Geographical Society included, as we have heard, a *pysanka* with an image of a fish. Relying on this single instance of *pysanka* 'ryba' [fish] one cannot make any conclusions about the symbolic meaning of this *pysanka* (though fish depicted in catacombs is a symbol of Christ). It is simpler to assume the random occurrence of this drawing.

There are *pysanky* in various places in Ukraine, Galicia [Halycnyna] and Poland named 'baraniachi rohy' [ram horns], 'kuriachi lapy' [hen feet], 'kachachi lapy' [duck feet], 'husiachi lapy' [goose feet], 'kachachi shyiky' [duck necks], 'zayachi vushky' [hare ears], with the corresponding figures, for example, four crossed lines with curved ends ('horns'), or three or four lines diverging from one point ('feet').

There were views expressed in the press regarding the influence of some ornamental patterns of carpets, fabrics and various decorations on *pysanka* ornaments. However, based on the collections and drawings known to us, we cannot agree with this opinion. We believe *pysanka* ornamentation to be original, in many cases traditional, and in many cases accidental – as a manifestation of a person's free aesthetic creativity, where local flora and various household items provide the imagery.

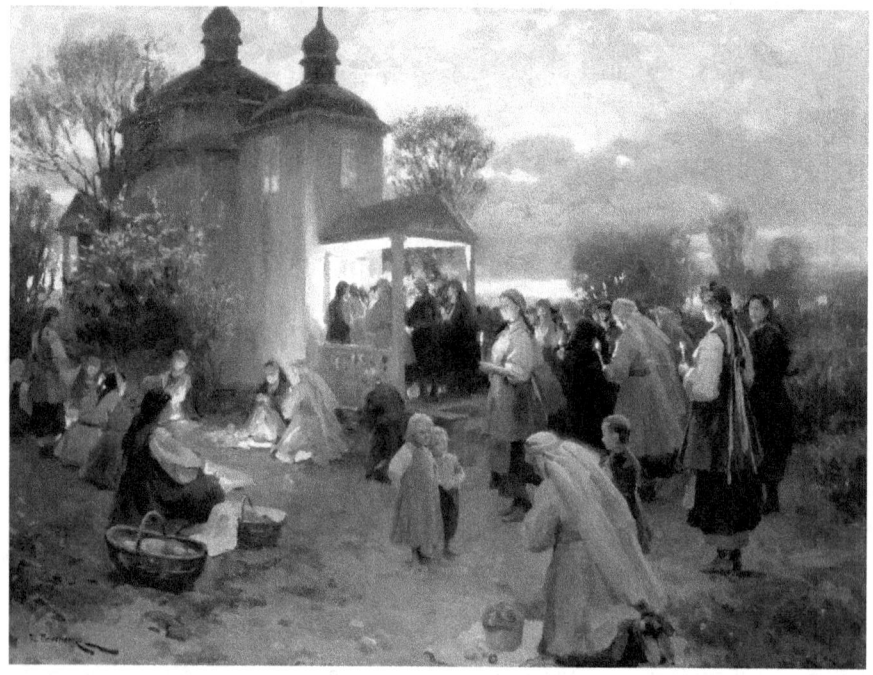

'Easter Sunrise Service' by Mykola Pymonenko (beginning of the 19th century).

Many *pysanka* symbols represent household objects. These *pysanky* include **'hrebin'** [comb], **'hrabli'** [rake], **'sokyra'** [axe], **'spletena strichka'** [intertwined ribbon], **'zontyk'** [umbrella] (in Galicia [Halychyna]), **'liulka'** [pipe] (in Kamianets-Podilskyi province), **'vovchi zuby'** [wolf teeth] (ibid), **'chovnyky'** [boats] **'sakvy'** [sacks], **'choboty'** [shoes], **'baklazhok'** [a flat vessel for water storage], **'skrypka'** [fiddle], **'bochonok'** [small barrel] and **'motovyltse'** [bobbin] (from Temriuk town, [Kuban region], which is quite similar to a Bulgarian *pysanka* from Dobruja).

In relation to the scevomorphic ornamentation, let us note the following: a *pysanka* named **'besahy'** is found in Kamianets-Podilskyi province and depicts red Moldovan **'besahy'** ('double-sack' [i.e. consisting of two sacks that are joined together], which is carried over the shoulder, where one sack rests on the chest and the other on the back) on a dark background. A similar pattern is found on *pysanka* from Barsukovska village, Kuban region.

Pysanky with the **'drabyna'** [ladder] ornament are made in Tenhinska village, Kuban region and in Kursk province (a Russian *pysanka* in my collection). The Polish **'drabyna'** [ladder] has nine or ten steps (Udziela 1888, p. 9).

Pysanky **'kalytky'** [purses] are found in various places in Ukraine. Priest Rodkevych from Kamianets-Podilskyi province offers an original assumption about the origin and significance of this ornament, which is used on *pysanky* in his province. Among the objects that are depicted on the icons of Christ's Passion, there is also Judas' money bag, which gives rise to the question of whether the *pysanka* **'kalytky'** [purses] represents Judas' bargaining

Scevomorphic symbols

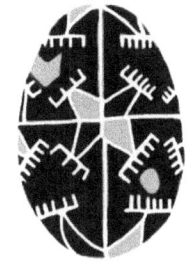

'Hrebinchyk' (also, 'hrebinets' [diminutive form of 'hrebin' (comb)] pysanka (Kulzhynskyi 1899, table 9, no. 7).

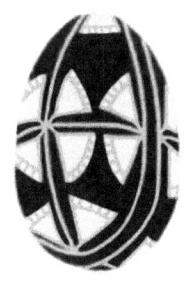

'Hrebinchyk' (also, 'hrebinets' [diminutive form of 'hrebin' (comb)] pysanka (Kulzhynskyi 1899, table 8, no. 16).

during the betrayal of the Saviour. *Pysanka* **'kalytochka'** [diminutive form of 'kalytka', singular of 'kalytky' (purses)] is also found in Kupyansk county, Kharkiv province.

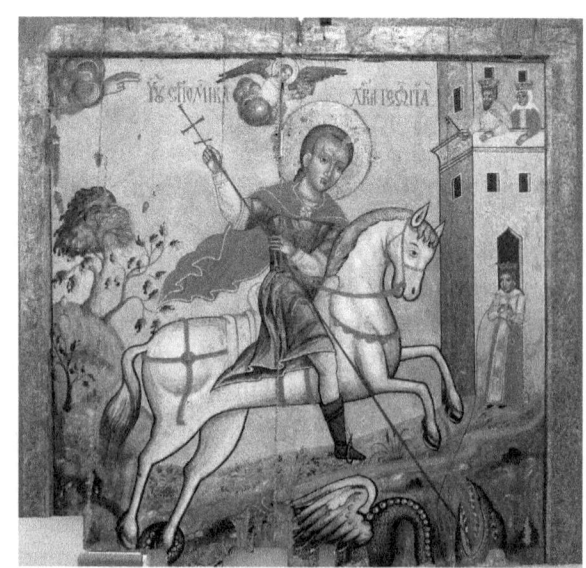

Icon of Saint George, artist unknown, origin Popeli village, Lviv region (second half of the 16th century).

In some places the custom of making *pysanky* on the occasion of Easter is about to disappear. In other places it has ceased to exist and elsewhere the custom has been greatly weakened. On my request to send *pysanky* and information about them, the famous ethnographer, Ivan Manzhura, replied to me: "In the last days of the Holy Week, as persistently as I was looking for *pysanky* at two Katerynoslav markets, there was not a trace of them. I also did not find any in the immediate vicinity of the city, although there the people still remember them, but the custom of making them has already died." Another esteemed researcher of folk life, Petro Ivanov, wrote to me: "In recent years, in Kupyansk town, they neither make *pysanky* any longer, as they did previously, nor do they sell them. The sugar and porcelain *pysanky* that are sold in the shop have ousted the home-made ones from use, although there are women still alive who used to make *pysanky* with their mothers and in previous years, during Great Lent, they used to sell hundreds of *pysanky*. 'There is no profit. It is not worth making them,' is their answer to my question of why they do not make *pysanky* now. On the outskirts of Kharkiv, just twenty years ago, they would still make *pysanky*, but now this custom has disappeared from here as well; and they limit themselves to simple *krashanky* or sugar and glass *pysanky* from the shop. Last year, during the Holy Week, at the markets I found four *pysanky* from Korotych village [Kharkiv county, Kharkiv province], which is located 15 versty [over 16 kilometres] from the city."

In other areas, the custodianship of the custom falls on an old woman, with whose death the last trace of the custom will vanish. Thus, the *pysanky* are made by a painter and an old woman in Anyno village, Lebedyn county;

Conclusion

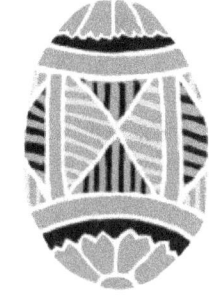

'Klynchasta' [meaning with drawn wedges] pysanka (Kulzhynskyi 1899, table 7, no. 10).

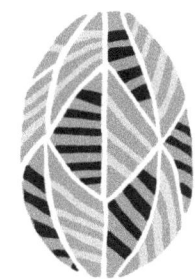

'Klynchasta' [meaning with drawn wedges] pysanka (Kulzhynskyi 1899, table 5, no. 16).

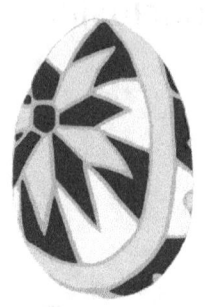

'Rozheva' [malva's] pysanka (Kulzhynskyi 1899, table 9, no. 4).

by an old man and an old woman in Boromlia village, Okhtyrka county; by an old woman, Aryna Holovchykha, in Ostroverhivka village, Kharkiv county; and an old woman, Akulyna Falenko, in Temriuk town [Kuban region].

The decline of the custom is dramatically revealed in the weakness and detriment of the pattern: the lines are uneven, and ornamentation is performed carelessly and roughly. The only instrument, the stylus, is abandoned, and they drop wax directly on an egg from the burning candle. As a result, *pysanky* from Kharkiv, Katerynoslav and Poltava regions are much rougher and blander than the Volyn and Kamianets-Podilskyi *pysanky* and weaker in execution than Polish and Czech ones. We think that one cannot base the disadvantages of *pysanky* from Left-bank Ukraine on its relatively eastern position, its remoteness from the western Slavs or from the rich (in artistic terms) sources of European culture. In fact, in Left-bank Ukraine as well as among the Russian population of Kursk province, one can come across *pysanky* that are rather elegant in drawing and bright in colour. However, they are found rarely and only in a few locations, like a fragment of the better state of the past *pysanka*-making art. Aesthetic sense and a love of elegance are no less a characteristic of the Ukrainian people than they are of the Western Slavic nations. The material collected by me is so small in a quantitative respect that it is not possible to identify either historical traditions or local influences on the *pysanka*-making art. Only professionally made *pysanky* are easily identified by their intricate designs (for example, 'perforated heart'), by the presence of gilding or by inscriptions. Collections of the villagers' *pysanky*, with the exception of some instances which are found ubiquitously (for example, 'bezkonechnyk' [eternity band]), are quite varied in the intensity and brightness of the colours, as well as in the predominance of one or the other colour, and in the choice of phytomorphic ornaments.

In conclusion of the article, I cannot help but express two wishes. The first wish is for our educated sector of society and people of science to pay serious attention to the dying custom of *pysanka*-making, to collect what else can be collected and to continue my current work on the basis of new materials. The second wish is for our people, through education, to further develop those rich artistic talents that they expressed in *pysanky*, in the elegance of their drawings, in the skilful selection of colours as well as in the purity and nobility of the whole *pysanka* ornamentation.

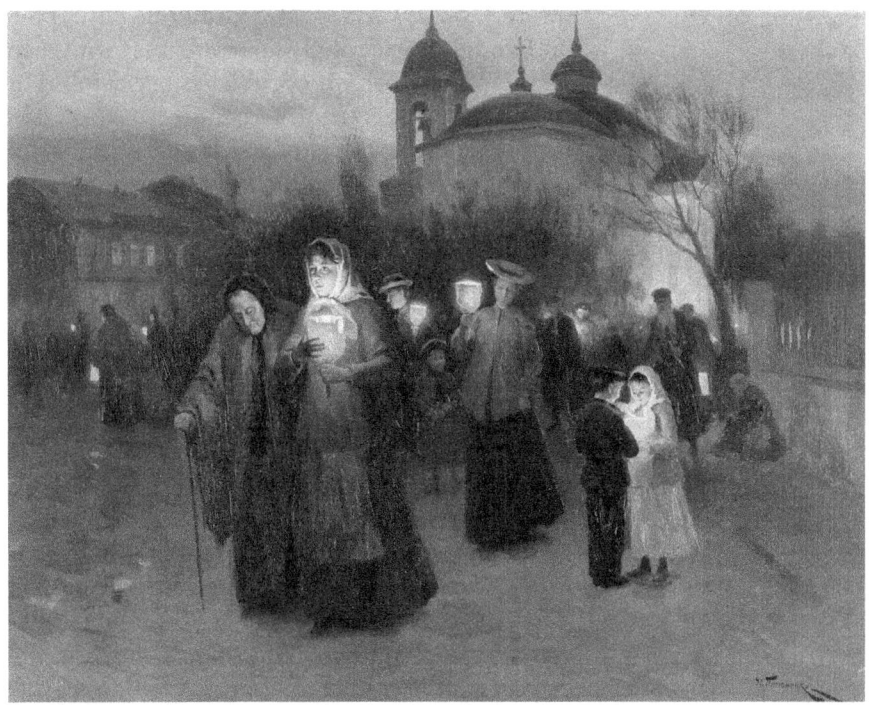

'Maundy Thursday' by Mykola Pymonenko (1887).

Additional information

Since this article has been in print, we have collected additional new materials that complement information already given about *pysanky*.

A message from a teacher, Mr Ivanyk from Kabardynsk village, Kuban region, stated that there they do not make *pysanky*, only *krashanky*. There are also no legends, proverbs or such. They make *krashanky* during Holy [Week] for Easter and then again for *Hrobky Week*. They do not keep eggshells. They dye the eggs in red, yellow, blue and black colours, which they purchase at a local shop.

Thanks to V. H. Filonov's kind assistance, I received 20 *pysanky* made by villagers from Balakliya village, Zmiiv county [Kharkiv province]. The *pysanky* are in tricolour with yellow and white drawings on red background. The drawings are pale and roughly executed. They are performed in geometric and phytomorphic styles. Several of them depict the four-armed Latin cross and one is **'bezkonechnyk'** [eternity band] (that is 14 white parallel lines on the red background).

In Smolensk province, there is a ritual of carrying religious icons during Easter. This ritual is performed by certain men, usually lively villagers, who are called 'God-bearers'. Such a 'God-bearer' can sometimes collect up to 200 eggs during Holy Week. He [a God-bearer] is also often a great enthusiast of the game 'bytky' [knocking eggs], and it often happens that with one egg he can win a whole dozen eggs. They often have a guineafowl egg, which is considered to be an all-destructing 'battering ram'. Sometimes a priest, deacon and sexton participate in the game of 'bytky' [knocking eggs] as well, and currently this game is quite popular among village youth. A 'stone' egg is strictly forbidden, and, under customary law, such an egg is often thrown at the head of its

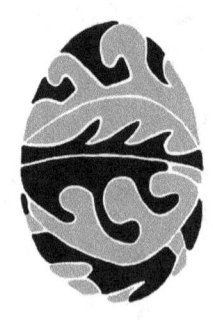

'Klenovyi lyst' [maple leaf] pysanka (Kulzhynskyi 1899, table 12, no. 7).

owner (*Smolenskiy Vestnik* [Smolensk Herald], republished in *Den* [Day] 1891, no. 1032).

Zygmunt Gloger indicated that the most ancient testimony of *pysanky* could be found as early as in the 13th century in [Wincenty] Kadłubek's *Chronicle* (Gloger 1891).

The same issue of *Wisła* (1891, vol. 5, book 1) published an excerpt from Milan Djakov Milićević's writings *Zivot Srba Seljaka* [Serbian peasant life] about pysanka-making in Serbia, and its similarity to pysanka-making in Ukraine (Ciszewski 1891).

A *pysanka* named **'besachy'** [double-sacks, see also **'besahy'**] depicts a Romanian double bag, which has been known to Romanians from ancient times. The Roman sources on 'bisaccium' are found in writings of Petronius (who died in 67 AD).

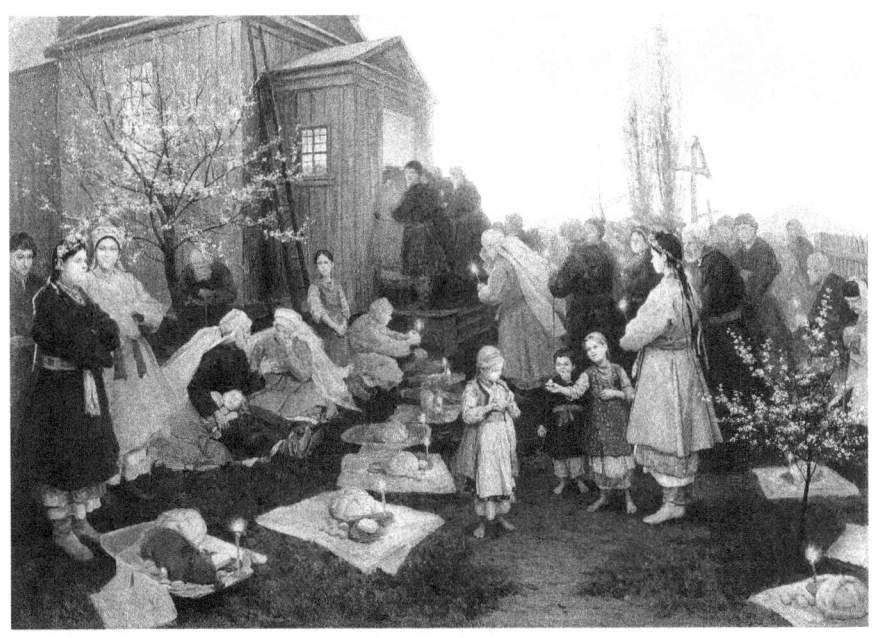

'Easter Morning Prayer' by Mykola Pymonenko (1891).

1889 Ritual Egg

Mykola Sumtsov

Mykola Sumtsov, an ethnographer, published this article on the Ukrainian ritual Easter eggs in Kievskaya Starina [*Kyivan Antiquity*] *in 1889 (He would publish a more extensive piece in the journal in 1891, nos. 5 and 6 – extracted here in chapter 'Pysanky'). In this article Sumtsov notes the symbolism of the 'red egg', the use of Easter eggs in social customs and as a talisman in folk superstitions, as well as the methods of egg decoration in different regions.*

Easter would not be a festive day without the red egg. After the morning mass, as soon as the priest has sprinkled each villager's modest goods with holy water, two or three eggs, accompanied by two or three *kopiyky*, are destined for the deacon's [alms] bag. The villagers exchange Easter greetings[1] and the red egg [red-dyed egg] changes hands. During the Holy Week people 'roll', 'knock'[2] and exchange the Easter eggs. To 'knock eggs' is an ancient ritual. The clergy opposed it in the 17th century, as they perceived in it something contrary to religion.

In some locations, on the first day of Easter the villagers place on the table a wooden pail with wheat grains in which an Easter egg has been buried. These grains are later sown. When sowing hemp, the villagers scatter the eggshell, saying, "God, bring forth hemp as

1. Easter greetings – one of the traditional Easter greeting rituals in Ukraine is called *khrystosuvannia*, see Glossary.

2. 'Roll', 'knock' – the author refers to folk games featuring Easter eggs. These games, under different names and in various versions, were popular among several Slavic peoples.

white as eggs!" On Ascension Thursday they go to the fields sown with rye and throw the red eggs upwards, to induce the rye to rise as high as the thrown egg. When on Saint George's Day they take their herds to the pastures, they stroke the horses' backs with the egg, saying, "As the egg is smooth and round, you too, my horse, be pretty and full". Holding the dyed egg, they walk around their herds to prevent wolves from attacking it. In some places they consider it to be useful to walk around a burning house with an Easter egg to stop fire from moving to neighbouring buildings. In the Valky district [Kharkiv region], they say that for this purpose one should use an egg that has been blessed [each Easter] over a period of three years.

There is a long history behind the honouring of the red egg: it is more ancient than Christianity. Pagans saw the red egg as a symbol of the sun, which, as is well-known, became their main object of worship. Honouring of the red egg initially originated from the concept of the sun's resurrection or, to be more precise, the whole creative power of nature. The hot summer Sun appeared to the Pagan Slavs in various guises: a divine face, a chariot, a ring and a bird. The folk tales often mention a *firebird*. This famous bird is, in fact, the spring and summer sun. One of its feathers is enough to illuminate a large garden. However, like all embodiments of the creative power, the *firebird* has its foes, which take the form of winter cold and snowstorms. A sorcerer abducts the *firebird*, but does not kill it (it is impossible to kill the creative power of nature that is eternally reborn each spring). Just before the precious bird loses its freedom, it manages to lay an egg. The Sun, enveloped in fog and clouds, seems to be a golden egg laid by that bird. With its hot rays it warms the cold clouds, dispels the fog, and makes clouds pour with flows of rain; fields and pastures turn green and the kingdom of summer settles upon the earth. The folk legends portray the egg as a source of life, and as the universe. According to Finnish legends, the universe originated from an egg: the sun [originated] from the egg white; the moon [originated] from the egg yolk; the sky [originated] from one half of the eggshell; and the earth [originated] from the other half. The ancient Persian people also believed in the creation of the universe from an egg. They praised the egg in their divine songs and kept iron figurines of eggs in their temples. The Greek and Roman philosophers also traced the origins of the universe to an egg (*ab ovo*).

The honouring of the red egg as a symbol of a strong and fruitful spring sun was timed with the Feast of the Resurrection of Jesus, because this Christian feast coincided with an ancient Pagan celebration of the rebirth of the creative power of nature.

Easter eggs are varied in their ornaments. The *pysanky* of the *Galician Rus* [Halychyna or Galicia, Ukraine] are made by women in the following manner. They apply wax to those areas [of the egg] that they want to keep white, and then they immerse the egg into apple bark brew, which gives a yellow colour to the egg. They achieve the basis or foundation in this way then they again apply wax to other spots and immerse the egg into one dye or another.

At the ethnographic exhibition in Kolomyia town, more than 800 *pysanky* were presented from various villages: Zahaypil, Khomyakivka, Chortovets, Herasymiv and others. *Pysanky* from Tekuche village were entirely dyed in yellow using Saint John's wort (*Hypericum perforatum*). The Polish ethnographers and archeologists also showed their interest in *Galician Rus* [Halychyna or Galicia, Ukraine] *pysanky*. Thus, the Krakow Academy of Sciences contains a small collection of *pysanky*. It appears that Ukrainian *pysanky* were exhibited in Vienna and Paris where they attracted the attention of scholars (Kolberg 1882).

Easter eggs are named according to their colour [and pattern]: 'tserkovtsi' [churches] are images of Greek style crosses; 'popovi ryzy' [priest vestment]; 'dzvin' [bell]; *'paska'* [a ritual Ukrainian Easter bread]; 'baraniachi rohy' [ram horns]; 'kvitky' [flowers]; 'kucheri' [curls]; and others.

Let us note here that customs, in addition to the ritual [Easter] eggs, include, among others, fried eggs. The fried eggs are predominantly present at weddings. It seems that the ritual fried eggs exist only in Galicia [Halychyna], namely at Lemkos' weddings, where they fry eggs for the newlyweds for supper. Here, as in many parts of Russia, the fried eggs have a direct connection with marriage.

1890

Skarzhynska's Museum in Lubny

Vasyl Horlenko

In 1890 Vasyl Horlenko, a biographer and ethnographer from Chernihiv region, Ukraine, focused on one of the notable collections of pysanky in the Skarzhynska Museum. His piece illuminates the work of a pioneering woman Kateryna Mykolaivna Skarzhynska, who produced an extraordinary collection, part of which still exists today, at a time when 'folk museums' were not widely valued.

[Extract]

Thanks to work and diligence of a few enlightened individuals, scientific collections of antiquities as well as of ancient household and cultural objects continue to appear alongside the archaeological, ethnographical and, naturally, historical collections, despite the astonishing and ignorant indifference that the district public institutions of our southern towns express towards the gathering and conservation of such collections.

One of the most exceptional collections of this kind belongs to a landowner of Lubny county, Poltava province, Kateryna Mykolaivna Skarzhynska, and has become known publicly in the last five or six years. [...] We are reporting on this collection after recently viewing it in its entirety on location (Kruhlyk khutir, near Lubny town). However, due to the variety of the museum's departments, and the novelty and appeal of some of them, this collection is in need of a more detailed description, which, without a doubt, will be presented when the collection becomes more famous and reaches the desired uniformity and completeness in all its components.

[...] It would be appropriate to note here how closely archaeology and ethnography are related in the *Southern Rus* [Ukraine]. The folk life, in its many aspects, has, for centuries, remained the foundation, on which the sorrowful events of *Southern Rus* [Ukrainian] history have been taking place one after another, but a strictly defined cycle of agricultural village lifestyle has, through its conservatism, preserved many features of antiquity up to the present day. In addition to that, this noblest class of our people summed up what expresses our nationality the most and it is here the most original manifestations of the distinctive genius of *Southern Rus* [Ukraine] have emerged. For that reason it is necessary for any historical and archaeological collection [undertaking] to turn to this source, that is our folk, which is the best testament of the past life.

When collecting items of cultural antiquity one often comes across imitations and replicas (in Western European, Polish and Eastern [styles]), as well as objects of purely foreign origin; whereas anything produced by the folk represents their spiritual assets, and was created by them, like the surroundings within which they live, and the songs they sing, and the bread they eat. The insignificant and – ostensibly – low-value items of people's everyday life embody the elements of their spiritual wealth, independent mind and taste.

Those who are interested in the art of ornamentation have long turned their attention to *pysanky*, the decoration of which, due to their solemn and festive as well as semi-sacred significance, is passed down in succession in immutable and archaic form. Last year the Lubny museum collected 300 [*pysanka*] specimens from Lubny and surrounding counties (mostly), as well as from the provinces of Kamianets-Podilskyi, Kyiv and Chernihiv and from Bessarabia; [the specimens] were accompanied by notations depicting the folk names of their symbols and the place of their production.

Whole series of *pysanky* were made to order, representing the entire repertoire of one master – such as the 70 *pysanky* from Nyzhniy Bulatets village, near Lubny. As well as some instances of decline, the opposite phenomena [the preservation of *pysanka*-making traditions] is apparent in this sector. In some places, in order to make their *pysanky* they buy aniline dyes in pharmacies; however, they continue to make *pysanky* according to the same old wax method (moreover, the professional artists also make their *pysanky* the same way). In most cases, nonetheless, vegetable dyes are used, which are extracted by the masters themselves. For her work, a woman in the village receives one egg and one *kopiyka*; at the markets she earns two *kopiyky*; and, when commissioned by the museum, [she receives] five *kopiyky*.

The names of the symbols as well as their shapes vary

considerably. Here are some of them: 'sorok klyntsiv' [forty wedges], 'klynchasta' [meaning *pysanka* with drawn wedges], 'bezkonechnyk' [eternity band], 'rozha' [mallow], 'povna rozha' [full mallow], 'sosna' [pine], 'pavuk' [spider], 'kalytochky' [diminutive form of 'kalytky' (purses)], 'sheludyva rozha' [meaning simplified design of 'mallow], 'hvozdyka' [carnation], 'skoropyska' [meaning *pysanka* with a quickly drawn ornament], 'sorochi lapy' [magpie feet], 'husiachi lapy' [goose feet], 'klenovyi lyst' [maple leaf], 'khmelyk' [hop], 'brunky' [buds], 'kachachi lapy' [duck feet], 'yastrebovi lapy' [hawk feet], 'shuliachi lapy' [falcon feet], 'kosytsi' [braids], 'baraniachi rohy' [ram horns], 'hrebin' [comb], 'kryvi poyasky' [curved belts], 'zastuptsi' [spades], 'zirkova' (zvizdchata) [star], 'baryltse' [cask], 'mytus-kvitka' [meaning mutually opposite positioned flowers], 'kryzhovi khresty' [cross-like crosses] and so on.

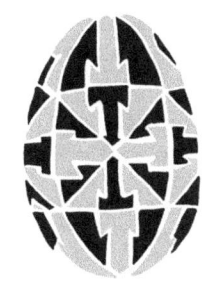

'Zastuptsi' [spades], pysanka (Kulzhynskyi 1899, table 13, no. 1).

The experience of the *pysanka*-collectors has established that, undoubtedly, certain types of drawings are spread across the whole region, but there are also patterns that a master combines during the actual drawing process. It can also happen that a name borrowed from a distant area is sometimes mistakenly applied to symbols of a different nature. These names should be checked by comparison. [...]

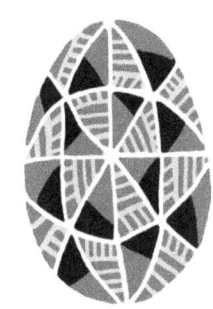

'Sorokoklyn' [forty wedges] pysanka (Kulzhynskyi 1899, table 5, no. 5).

1895

A Few Words on Pysanky

Volodymyr Yastrebov

Archaeologist and ethnographer Volodymyr Yastrebov examines the connections between Ukrainian, Bulgarian and Moldovan pysanka patterns and names, drawing attention to the possible origins of common Easter egg patterns.

Science barely touches on the ornamentation of Ukrainian *pysanky*, or on Ukrainian ornamentation in general. A person wishing to pursue this topic encounters obstacles along his path that are difficult to resolve. There are few collections of *pysanky* and those collections are scattered and are in private hands. To publish them in colour, in the present circumstances of the printing business, is very expensive. As a result, there are very few illustrations that offer a satisfactory depiction [of *pysanka*]. Also, nowhere has material been collected in sufficient detail for a comparative study of patterns on *pysanky*. Where, for example, can one study the patterns of embroidery, carpets and so on? And that is not all. *Pysanky*, and in particular their patterns, do not exclusively belong to Ukrainian culture. Therefore, a researcher ought to get acquainted with various foreign publications

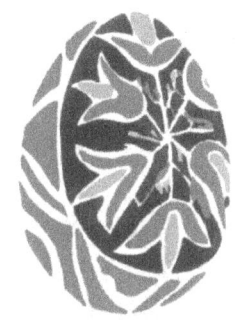

'Tiulpan' [tulip] pysanka (Kulzhynskyi 1899, table 13, no. 6) & (Rybalko 2010, table 3, no. 4).

1. Elysavethrad – is a
superseded name of
Kropyvnytskyi town,
Ukraine.

on ornamentations, despite of how scattered they are, especially those published by the southern Slavs and Romanians – although, apparently, those areas are not rich in resources either. Needless to say, in this article we are not setting such broad objectives for ourselves. We only want to share some observations, using the collection of *pysanky* that is at our disposal. This collection, which was created thanks to the donations made by the students at the Historical and Geographical Museum at the Elysavethrad[1] Realschule (Kherson province), contains almost 400 specimens of the *pysanky* from the provinces of Kherson [Ukraine], Kyiv [Ukraine], Podolsk [Russia], Chernihiv [Ukraine] and Bessarabia [Moldova]. However, the main core of the collection consists of *pysanky* from Kherson province, mainly from Elysavethrad and Oleksandria counties and then Ananiyiv and partly Odesa counties (from Beykush village near Ochakiv town). The distinctive feature of our collection is that, along with the predominantly greater quantity of Ukrainian *pysanky*, it also contains Bulgarian and Moldovan specimens, which gives some insight into the mutual influence of nationalities living here. Unfortunately, most of the specimens have no accompanying explanatory information, such as indications of the pattern names or of the nationality of the people from whom the *pysanky* were obtained, which, without a doubt, makes it impossible for us to make broader and more solid conclusions.

Let us focus mainly on the names of the symbols. In the north of the Kherson province, the most dominant symbols on Ukrainian *pysanky* are those that are popular throughout the rest of Ukraine, including in Galicia [Halychyna]: 'baraniachi rozhky' [ram horns], 'bezkonechnyk' [eternity band], 'besahy' [double-sack], 'bokova rozha' [side mallow],

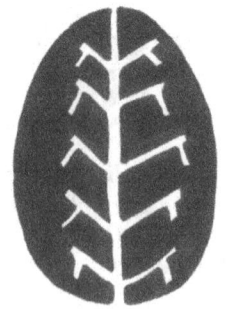

A Moldovan pysanka (Kulzhynskyi 1899, table 13, no. 13) & (Rybalko 2010, table 6, no. 1).

'bochka' [barrel], 'vynohrad' [grapevine], 'vytushka' [meaning a curl], 'hvozdyka' [carnation], 'hrebin' [comb], 'husiachi lapy' [goose feet], 'dubovyi lyst' [oak leaf], 'zastuptsi' [spades], 'zirka' [star], 'kalytky' [purses], 'z krapynkamy' [with speckles], 'kruti rozhky' [curved horns], 'kryltsia' [wings], 'kuriachi lapy' [hen feet], 'lastovyni khvostyky' [swallow tails], 'lystiachka' [leaves], 'lomanyi khrest' [broken cross], 'ohirkove ohudynnia' [climbing cucumber vine], 'pavuk' [spider], 'povna rozha' [full mallow], 'sobacha rozha' [marsh mallow], 'sorok klyntsiv' [forty wedges], 'sorocha lapka' [magpie foot] and 'khrest' [cross].

In addition to that, among the names of Ukrainian *pysanky* in our collection, we have found a few of those that previously were not mentioned as belonging to the Ukrainian *pysanky*[2]: 'vazonchyk' [flowerpot], 'pererva' [break], 'choboty' [boots], 'tiulpany' [tulips], 'uhlushky' [angles], 'khrystata rozha' [cross-like mallow] and 'shist kvitok' [six flowers].

The names of many Moldovan *pysanky* are identical to the Ukrainian ones or present a literal translation of the letter, such as: 'baraniachi rohy' [ram horns], 'husiacha lapka' [goose foot], 'kosychata rozha' [means, asymmetrical and horizontal mallow], 'lomanyi khrest' [broken cross], 'povna rozha' [full mallow], 'sorok klyntsiv' [forty wedges], 'sosonka' [diminutive form of 'sosna' (pine tree)], 'khrest' [cross] and 'sheludyva rozha' [meaning simplified design of mallow].

For just two of the [Moldovan] *pysanky* we were unable to find the corresponding names in Ukrainian [*pysanka*] terminology, although the words are Ukrainian: 'dyvok' and 'zalizo do pluha' (Mold., 'sheruplugului'; Engl., 'iron for plough'). [...]

Thus, most of the Bulgarian and Moldovan pysanka names coincide with

2. We refer to the following articles, 'Lubenskiy muzey K. N. Skarzhinskoy', *Kievskaya Starina* vol. XXXI [Horlenko 1890] and M. F. Sumtsov's article on pysanky, *Kievskaya Starina*, vol. XXXIII [Sumtsov 1891]. (Note from the author.)

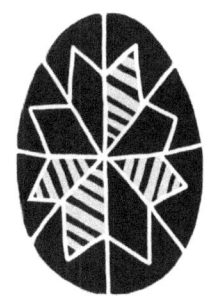

'Sheludyva rozha' [simplified design of full mallow] pysanka (Kulzhynskyi 1899, table 12, no. 4) & (Rybalko 2010, table 2, no. 2).

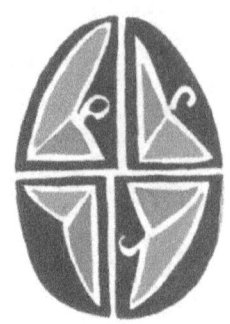

'Lastovyni khvostyky'
[swallow tails] pysanka
(Kulzhynskyi 1899,
table 12, no. 9) & (Rybalko
2010, table 1, no. 2).

3. *Kievskaya Starina,* vol.
XXXIII, p. 376 [Sumtsov
1891]. (Note from the
author.)

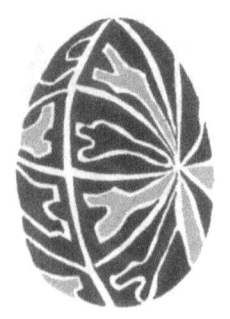

'Choboty' [boots] pysanka
(Kulzhynskyi 1899,
table 7, no. 8).

Ukrainian ones. Local Bulgarians argue that both the custom of making *pysanky*, and their names, are indigenous to them, and that they did not borrow them from anywhere, and that their isolation, which distinguishes them in relation to other peoples around them, is proof of it. Therefore, a question arises as to whether in this case the Ukrainians and Moldovans borrowed [*pysanka* names] from the Bulgarians, perhaps even much earlier in the 18th century, when Bulgarians began to settle on Ukrainian territory. As for the Moldovans, on our territories relations between them and Ukrainians – and in particular crosscultural marriages – are well known. Therefore we are inclined to think that Moldovans borrow *pysanka* names from Ukrainians, especially keeping in mind that most of the time they retain the Ukrainian pronunciation, whereas the Bulgarians have all the *pysanka* names in Bulgarian.

Among Ukrainian symbols there is one which we found that was not among the *pysanky* in Kateryna Skarzhynska's Museum in Lubny nor in Professor Sumtsov's research [Sumtsov 1891]. This symbol is named 'tiulpany' [tulips]. However, in Sumtsov's article we found an indication that a *pysanka* with this pattern is known to Serbs.[3] Perhaps this pattern is the remainder of the last century New Serbia, located exactly in the area of our observations.

Pysanka patterns are not completely isolated from the patterns of other objects. Of course, the mere shape of the object to a large extent determines the content of the ornament. However, at the same time, among the *pysanka* patterns one can identify those that are popular, for example, in embroidery. These are: 'vazonchyk' [flowerpot], 'vynohrad' [grapevine], 'hvozdyka' [carnation], 'zirochka'

[star], 'kruti rozhky' [curved horns], 'povna rozha' [full mallow], 'sobacha rozha' [marsh mallow], 'sosonka' [diminutive form of 'sosna' (pine tree)] and 'khrest' [cross].[4]

Credible sources have informed us that *pysanka* patterns are also borrowed from carpet designs.

In our localities the pysanka background for the most part is black, orange-red and sometimes white. The drawing is performed most often in three colours: red, yellow and white, and more rarely in two or four colours. In addition to those mentioned, green and black dyes are also used. Red is used in various shades: pink, crimson or magenta. There is no noticeable difference in the dyeing of the *pysanky* among the Ukrainians, Moldovans and Bulgarians. Some Moldovan *pysanky* from Bessarabia, which are available in our collection, are almost all of one colour – pink. More rarely they are crimson, with a white pattern, which is very original in design.

4. *Trudy Tretiego Arkheologicheskogo Sjezda (v Kieve)* [Works of the Third Archaeological Congress (in Kyiv)], vol. 2, pp. 321–322, and illustrations 28, 30, 73, 76 and so on [Volkov 1878]. (Note from the author.)

1897   A Collection of Pysanka Patterns

The anonymous author's article offers a review of the upcoming book dedicated to Kateryna Skarzhynska's collection of pysanky (Kulzhynskyi 1899). It includes some valuable observations on the process of collecting pysanky, publishing the designs for posterity and the printing processes available at that time.

Some time ago *Kievskaya Starina* [*Kyivan Antiquity*] reported on Kateryna Skarzhynska's intended publication containing drawings of *pysanky*. Back in 1895 Kateryna Skarzhynska's Lubny Museum [Poltava region] had published a booklet in which the museum reported that it has a large collection of *pysanky* (more than a thousand exhibits). The museum invited 'all folk art aficionados' to help them in furthering the expansion of the collection by sending in more exhibits.

    The booklet offered detailed instructions on collecting *pysanky* and all kinds of information about them. To some collectors these instructions may perhaps have seemed overly detailed. It was recommended that accompanying the *pysanky* there should be information on who, where, when, under what circumstances, using what method and

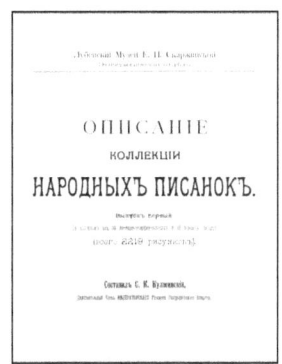

(Kulzhynskyi 1899).

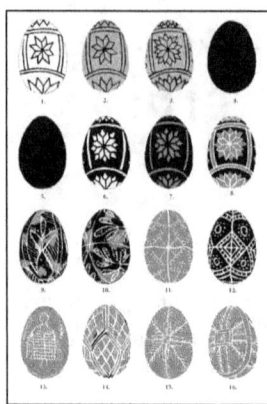

Pysanky, Table 1,
(Kulzhynskyi 1899).

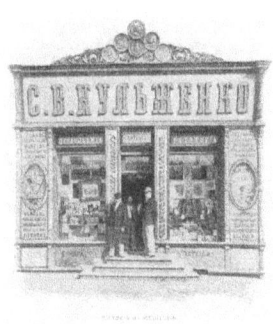

Stefan Kulzhenko's
building on
Khreshchatyk Street, Kyiv.

instruments and for what purpose the *pysanka* was made but a wish was also expressed to even know the social and marital status of the master from whom the *pysanka* had been acquired ... The instructions also stated that 'negative responses have a value almost equal to the positive ones for the museum' (?), and that 'if it is not always possible to give answers even to a few of the offered questions, even such an impossibility will be significant for the museum...'

It would be very interesting to know how many correspondents were found by the museum, how many *pysanky* and related information have been sent in. No matter how – whether by drawing information from the extant materials or by supplementing it with the newly received information – Kateryna Skarzhynska has embarked on a big chromolithographic publication of *pysanka* patterns.

We were able to see the first two tables of this *Collection* [Kulzhynskyi 1899], which have been already printed. Leaving a more detailed report until the release of the entire *Collection* [Kulzhynskyi 1899], we will now say a few words about these initial tables. Each table is represented on a fairly large page, which contains 16 lithographic life-size images of *pysanky* in the appropriate colours. Next to some *pysanky*, those parts of a pattern that could not be fitted in the image are placed separately.

The publication promises to be very impressive: we are told that it will consist of thirty such tables. Its content is also impressive – the gathered material is extensive and diverse, which was expected, as the *pysanka* patterns for the *Collection* [Kulzhynskyi 1899] were gathered from thirteen provinces. However, if the collection was accrued from such a large area, it is likely that the patterns belong to a population which is represented by a number of nationalities. If so, then this needs to be elaborated on in the footnotes, otherwise the merit of the material will, to a large degree, be lost.

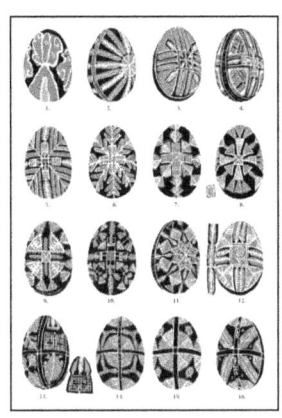

Pysanky, Table 2,
(Kulzhynskyi 1899).

For all the undoubted diversity of materials in Kateryna Skarzhynska's *Collection* [Kulzhynskyi 1899], there will obviously be many variants of the same motifs, which can be seen already from the first two tables. Thus, the first table contains an image of a *pysanka* flower pattern (called 'povna rozha' [full mallow]), which is presented eight times; certain images vary only in colouring, for example, one image depicts red 'rozha' [mallow] on a brown background, another image has a green flower on the same background, a third has exactly the same pattern and background – but features a white flower and so on. We do not know for what audience exactly the *Collection* [Kulzhynskyi 1899] is intended. If they have in mind members of the general public who buy 'patterns' in general, then to such an audience the choices of the *Collection* [Kulzhynskyi 1899] may seem monotonous; also since pattern variants increase the size of publication, and consequently the price of its copies, the *Collection* may end up being too expensive.

However if the *Collection* [Kulzhynskyi 1899] is designed for professionals, academics and ethnographers, then they will greatly thank Kateryna Skarzhynska, as an abundance of pattern variants will provide an opportunity to judge both the degree of popularity of the well-known pattern and the details of its variations. This is observed in studies of verbal ethnographic materials (folk tales and songs); the same should be studied, of course, in the area of ornamentation. The only necessary point

1. Author refers to Tovarishchestvo Skoropechatni A. A. Levensona [A. A. Levenson Printery] (1881–1917) in Moscow.

2. Stefan Kulzhenko (1837–1906) was one of the most successful and innovative printers in the 19th century Eastern Europe.

3. It is most likely that the author refers to O. Kosach's book *Ukrainskiy Narodnyi Ornament* [Ukrainian Folk Ornament], which was printed in S. Kulzhenko's printing house in 1876 (Kosach 1876).

to add is that if the *Collection* [Kulzhynskyi 1899] is meant to be an ethnographic work, it is necessary for it to be systematic.

As for its appearance, judging by the first tables the *Collection* [Kulzhynskyi 1899] will look quite good. It is printed on good thick paper; the paint is also of good quality. However, the lithography execution is a little rough and not sharp, to which we recommend the publisher to turn her attention, and also, when printing the following tables, to keep in mind that the outline of some *pysanky* is not quite smooth (nos. 4, 5 and 7 in the 1st table and no. 1 in the 2nd table). The inscriptions on some *pysanky*, which are of great interest, are made so indistinctly that it would take a long time to make out whether it is an inscription, or some incidental ornament. We advise the repeating of all the inscriptions in print in the notes.

One cannot but regret that Kateryna Skarzhynska's publication is printed not in Kyiv but in a Moscow printing house.[1] It is conceivable that such a printing house as one of Mr Kulzhenko[2] would have done the same job better, because twenty years ago Mr Kulzhenko printed *pysanky's* images[3] much more elegantly and clearly; furthermore, during these twenty years Mr Kulzhenko's lithography has been further refined.

The fact that the *Collection* of Kateryna Skarzhynska [Kulzhynskyi 1899] is printed in Moscow alerts us to potential [spelling] errors: some *pysanky* in their inscriptions include words 'ково' and 'тово', like in 'каво люблю, таво дарю' [whom I love, to him/her I gift]. Such phonetics are unusual in Ukrainian *pysanky*. Is it not, so to say, an error of a Moscow lithographer? The fact that such mistakes are possible in Moscow printing houses are evidenced by an example: we happened to read in the text cited under one illustration accompanying a famous Ukrainian song that was printed by one of Moscow's best printing house: 'військо йде, коровоньки мають'... [an army marches with its *cows*]; it should be 'короговки' [flags] instead of 'коровоньки' [cows]: 'an army marches with its *flags*'. Obviously, a Kyiv editor would not have missed it, whereas the Moscow one decided that: 'perhaps it should be like that there ...' Therefore we advise paying more attention to all the aspects related to printing of the *Collection* [Kulzhynskyi 1899] in the Moscow printing house.

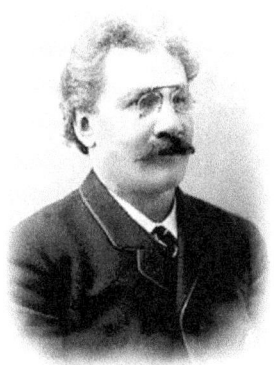

Stefan Kulzhenko.

This is all that can be said about the first sample tables of the *Collection* [Kulzhynskyi 1899]. We restate that, in general, its appearance is rather good, and its content is rich and interesting, thus the publication of Kateryna Skarzhynska promises to be a very valuable asset to our ethnographers.

1898   Krashanky in the Old Days

Matviy Nomys

In 1898 Matviy Nomys wrote about the games and rituals associated with Easter eggs in literary references and recalled associated customs from his childhood and youth in the 1820s and 1830s.

In Oleksandr Lazarevskyi's story about a quarrel between Osyp Hamaley and the priest Kantarovskyi (Lazarevskyi 1875, p. 444), Hamaley's words are cited as follows: "on Easter holidays we hit 'riadky' [rows (of eggs)] with boiled eggs and then we ate those 'riadky' [rows (of eggs)] together." A footnote to Hamaley's words contains Kantarovskyi's clarification: "On Easter holidays I did not hit the rows with him, but I hit the red eggs." The author then makes the following comment: "Hitting rows of eggs probably constituted some custom, of which we now know nothing about."

It is possible that subsequently the author or someone else found information about these 'rows'; however, I believe it not insignificant to report how in Zarih village,[1] during my childhood (in the 1820s to 1830s)

1. Zarih – Zarih village, Lubny county, is the birthplace of the author of this article. (Note from the editor of *Kievskaya Starina* [Kievan Antiquity].)

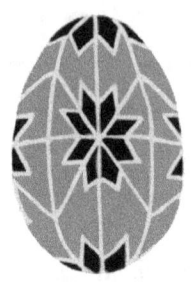

*'Zirka' [star] pysanka
(Kulzhynskyi 1899,
table 9, no. 1).*

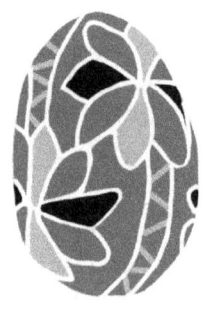

*'Zvizdy' [stars] pysanka
(Kulzhynskyi 1899,
table 6, no. 13).*

on Easter holidays (mainly, on the first day [of celebrations]) we enjoyed games involving eggs.

At Easter the following eggs were in use: *krashanky* dyed in red; in dark-blue with a special tint, and in yellow; the most popular were red, then dark-blue, and lastly yellow. *Krashanky* were not always boiled very hard, but the white [not dyed] eggs were always cooked hard-boiled.

We played with eggs two ways: 1) 'navbytky ([a game], which is not yet completely obsolete) is played exclusively with dyed, predominantly red eggs; and 2) 'kotiuchky' ([a game], which is now rarely in use) is played with (very hard-boiled) *krashanky* and with white [not dyed] eggs (from the long use in the game the eggs become soft like balls). One person puts his egg on a smooth surface, such as a well-trodden footpath. The other player rolls his egg very fast, from a certain distance, and if his egg touches the opponent's one, he [the 'roller'] takes it; if the outcome is contrary, then he loses his own egg ... If Kantarovskyi's 'riadky' [rows] are similar to 'kotiuchky', then Kantarovskyi's 'riadky' [rows] uses something like 'parlay', although I do not remember parlay in 'kotiuchky': it seems that in 'kotiuchky' we always played one on one.

1903   A Few Words on How to Make Pysanky and Krashanky

In 1903 Kievskaya Starina *[Kyivan Antiquity] published an article by an unknown author who wrote about methods used to make pysanky and krashanky in the counties of Balta and Ananiyiv, Kherson province.*

As it is known, nowhere is Easter celebrated so solemnly as it is here in Ukraine. Among all those foods that adorn the Ukrainian festive table, the eggs draw particular attention. They are the first to be eaten at *rozhovyny* [first ritual meal after Great Lent] and they are decorated and dyed in a variety of ways. Here is what I was able to learn about the ways in which *pysanky* and *krashanky* are made. This information refers to Balta town and its county as well as to part of Ananiyiv county, Kherson province.

Krashanky are dyed entirely in any one colour. The colour of the dye is usually red, yellow, green, dark-blue, purple and – rarely – black. In the city and in suburban villages they use aniline dyes, which are purchased in the shops. However, off the beaten path in country areas, where aniline dyes are hard to obtain, they enjoy homemade dyes, the recipe of which was probably handed down from their grandfathers. The yellow dye is an actual onion-peel broth. This broth is called 'zhovtvylo' [derived from 'zhovtyi', meaning 'yellow' in Ukrainian]. An infusion of sandalwood shavings on water, to which alum is added, is used instead of black and red manufactured dyes. *Krashanky* are usually boiled first and then dyed.

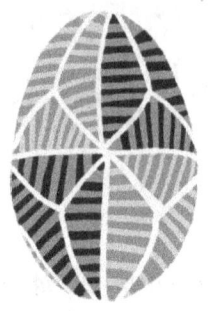

'Klyntseva' pysanka [meaning with drawn wedges] (Kulzhynskyi 1899, table 6, no. 9).

The making of *pysanky* is much more complex. As the name suggests, they are 'rozpysani' – ornamented by drawing. The tool for this purpose is a stylus: a stick with a piece of rolled-up thin metal sheet or foil attached to its end. At first, a (raw) egg is covered with melted wax using the stylus. Thus, under the wax, parts that are not supposed to be dyed according to the design (borders and rims), will remain undyed, and appear white. Then the egg is dipped into the dye and allowed to dry. After that those places that are supposed to preserve the colour [of this dye] are coated with wax.

The same technique is carried out with other dyes. The only principle observed is dipping into light colours first, and then into dark, because the dark dye is applied better on the light.

In relation to design, all *pysanky* are divided into two main categories: '*pysanky*-maliovanky' [*pysanky* with drawn ornament] and '*pysanky*-kopanky'. The latter have a lot of 'kapky' ('spots') in a variety of colours on a dark (usually black) background. The following symbols are distinguished in '*pysanky*-maliovanky': 'slyvky' [plums], 'orlyni kryltsia' [eagle wings], 'kuriachi lapy' [hen feet], 'dubove lystiachko' [oak leaf], 'sorok klyntsiv' [forty wedges], 'zvizda' [star], 'rozha' [mallow], 'hrabelky' [rake], 'ryba' [fish], 'vazonchyk' [flowerpot], 'pavuk' [spider], 'chornohuziachi kryltsia' [stock wings], 'lomani khresty' [broken crosses] and 'vyla' [pitchfork].

Once the whole ornament is executed, the eggs are baked in a bowl in a not-too-hot oven to remove the wax.

They begin to make *pysanky* at the end of the third and the beginning of the fourth week of Great Lent. The *pysanky* are usually drawn by old women and girls, rarely by adult women

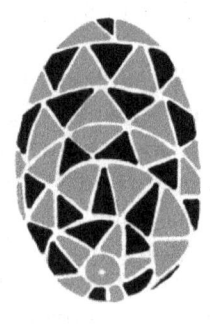

'Malenki klyntsi' [small wedges] pysanka (Kulzhynskyi 1899, table 9, no. 2).

and even more rarely by specialist artists. In the past there used to be quite a lot of them, and now there are none left at all, as I was told.

The *pysanky* that are left over from Easter are kept up until *Rakhmanskyi Velykden* (also known as Feast of Mid-Pentecost), when they are placed on water (if there is a river nearby) to float to *Rakhmany*.

There is also another use found for them, namely, in the priests' house-keeping, where *pysanky* are subjected to intense heat in huge cauldrons in the overheated ovens. The yolk thus receives the colour of a red-hot walnut, but nonetheless it is still edible, whereas the egg white becomes inedible. The baked eggs can be stored for 2–3 months. Usually in the summer these eggs are fed to hired help, such as the reapers from Polissia.

1904

About Krashanky and Pysanky

Hrepachevskyi A.

A. Hrepachevskyi's brief article presents a few folk beliefs and tales featuring the krashanky and pysanky. The lore, according to the footnote that accompanied the original publication, was collected from the small village of Miziakivski Khutory in Vinnytsia county, Podillia region and focused on some of the Judeo-Christian associations and superstitions connected with the Easter eggs.

1. When the Kings came to Christ with their gifts of myrrh and frankincense, Saint Mary Magdalene, who was very poor and had nothing to bring, took two eggs – she dyed one and drew [ornaments] on another – and brought them to Christ.

2. When Christ was on his way to crucifixion, non-believers teased him. They put rocks in a sheet and asked him to guess what they were hiding in the sheet. Christ told them: "[something] dyed and drawn on". They were ready to laugh at him, but when they opened the sheet they saw *krashanky* and *pysanky*. From that time onwards a custom originated to draw on and dye eggs.

3. Three Jewish women were on their way to a fair to sell their eggs. One of them put her basket with the eggs on the ground and fell asleep next to it. When she woke up, there were *pysanky* and *krashanky*.

4. If, for seven years, you use the same tablecloth to carry food [to the church] to be blessed at Easter and do not wash it, then this tablecloth acquires great power, with the help of which one can see *a fern flower* and hidden treasures. They say that one man from Dashkivtsi village, Lityn county, took his tablecloth, in which he carried *paska* to be blessed [each Easter] for seven years, his blessed knife, plate and Bible, and on the eve of *Green Week*, he went into the forest to see how *fern flower* blossoms. He put down the tablecloth, the plate, the Bible on the plate and a knife near the plate, and started reading the Bible. When midnight approached and a storm arose howling, whistling and bending trees almost to the ground, shivers ran down the man's spine. But he should not have become scared, because if one gets scared, he will not be able to see the *fern flower*. The very same moment the storm ended as well.

5. Whoever dies during Easter Week, goes to heaven, because the gateway to heaven is open that whole week.

6. They start making *pysanky* after *Khrestopoklonna Nedilia*, when churches bring out the crosses. On the Feast Day of the Forty Martyrs, one should make 'sorok klyntsiv' [forty wedges] design *pysanka*, whereas one should abstain from *pysanky* making on Palm Sunday and the Feast of the Annunciation. In order for *pysanky* to last long, they should be cooked on Maundy Thursday ... The yolk of the blessed egg is dried, then powdered and put on one's eyes, if they suffer from leucoma.

Bibliography

Afanasyev, A 1865–69, *Poeticheskie Vozzrenia Slavian na Prirodu* [The Slavs' Poetic Views on Nature], (in 3 vols.), K Soldatenkov, Moscow.

Beauplan, de G 1651, *Description des contrés du Royaume de Pologne* [Description of lands of the Kingdom of Poland] (1st ed.), *Description d'Ukranie, qui sont plusieurs provinces du Royaume de Pologne. Contenues depuis les confins de la Moscovie, insques aux limites de la Transilvanie* [Description of Ukraine, or Regions of the Kingdom of Poland between Muscovy and Transylvania], Chez Iacqves Cailloüe, dans la Cour du Palais, Rouen.

Bosyi, O & Bosa, L 2005, 'Doslidnyk stepovoi Ukrainy' [Explorer of steppe Ukraine], *Narodna Tvorchist ta Etnohrafiya* [Folk Art and Ethnography], no. 3, pp. 105–109.

Braker, N 2005, 'Volodymyr Mykolaevych Yastrebov. (Do trydtsiatykh rokovyn smerty)' [Volodymyr Mykolaevych Yastrebov. (On occasion of thirtieth anniversary of his death)], in S Yanchukov (ed.), *Z Imenem Volodymyra Yastrebova* [With the name of Volodymyr Yastrebov], Tsentralno-Ukrainske Vydavnytstvo [Central Ukrainian Publishing], Kirovohrad, pp. 4–24.

Brinton, D 1889, 'The ta ki, swastika, and cross in America', [in Bibligraphy], *Wisła*, vol. 4, book 3, pp. 708–712.

Carnoy, E & Nicolaides, J 1889,*Traditions Populaires de l'Asie Mineure* [Popular Traditions of Asia Minor], Maisonneuve & Ch. Leclerc, Paris.

Ch., L 1899, 'Nekroloh' [Obituary], *Zapysky Naukovoho Tovaryshchestva Imeni Shevchenka* [Notes of the Shevchenko Scientific Society], vol. 29, pp. 1–4.

Child, F 1882–98, *The English and Scottish Popular Ballads*, (in 5 vols.), Houghton, Mifflin and Company, Boston and New York.

Christmann, Fr & Oberländer, R 1873, *Ozeanien, die Inseln der Südsee* [Oceania, the Islands of the South Seas], Spamer, Leipzig.

Chubynskyi, P 1872–78, *Trudy Etnografichesko-Statisticheskoy Ekspeditsii v Zapadno-Russkiy kray* [Works of the Ethnographic-Statistical Expedition to the Western Rus Lands], (in 7 vols.), Maikov, Saint Petersburg.

Chykalenko, L 1923, 'Narys rozvytku heometrychnoho ornamentu paleolitychnoi doby' [Essay on development of the geometric ornament of the Paleolithic period], *Naukovyi Zbirnyk Ukrainskogo Universytetu v Prazi* [Scientific Anthology of Prague Ukrainian University], Prague Ukrainian University, vol. 1, pp. 148–200.

Ciszewski, S 1891, 'Pisanki w Serbji' [Pysanky in Serbia], *Wisła*, vol. 5, book 1, p. 167.

Cosquin, E 1886, *Contes Populaires de Lorraine* [Popular Tales of Lorraine], Vieweg, Paris.

Dmytrenko, M 2004, 'Vydatnyi ukrainskyi narodoznavets Mykola Sumtsov' [Mykola Sumtsov, a prominent Ukrainian ethnographer], *Narodna Tvorchist ta Etnohrafiya* [Folk Art and Ethnography], no. 3, pp. 3–15.

Dowgird, T 1890, 'Pisanki', *Wisła*, vol. 4, book 4, pp. 818–825.

Drahomanov, M 1876, *Malorusskie Narodnye Predania i Rasskazy* [Ukrainian Folk Legends and Stories], (in 2 vols.), Izdanie Yugo-Zapadnogo Otdela Imperatorskogo Russkogo Geograficheskogo Obshchestva [South-Western Division of Russian Imperial Geographical Society], Kyiv.

Erdmann, J 1736, *Commentatio Critica de Ovo Paschali* [Critical Studies on Easter Egg], Langenheim, Leipzig.

Glik, L 1889, 'Tetoviranje kože kod katolika u Bosni i Hercegovini od dra Leopolda Glika' [Catholics' tattoos in Bosnia and Herzegovina, by Dr Leopold Glik] *Glasnik Zemaljskog Muzeja Bosne i Hercegovine* [Herald of the National Museum of Bosnia and Herzegovina], year 1, book 3, pp. 81–88.

Gloger, Z 1891, 'Najdawniejszą wiadomość o pisankach' [The earliest information about pysanky], *Wisła*, vol. 5, book 1, pp. 166–167.

Gonzenbach, L 1870, *Sicilianische Märchen* [Sicilian Folk Tales], (in 2 vols.), W. Engelmann, Leipzig.

Granstrem, E (trans.) 1881, *Kalevala: Finskiy Narodnyi Epos* [Kalevala: Finnish Folk Epic], V. S. Balashev, Saint Petersburg.

Havelkova, V, Stranecka, F, Wankel, J & Wanklova, M 1888, *Moravske Ornamenty* [Moravian Ornaments], Vlastenecký Muzejní Spolek, Olomouc.

Heinecke, H 1889, 'Coutumes de Paques: Quelques Coutumes Allemandes' [Easter customs: some German customs], *Revue des Traditions Populaires* [Journal of Popular Traditions], vol. 4, pp. 351–352.

Horlenko, V 1890, 'Lubenskiy muzey K. N. Skarzhinskoy' [K. M. Skarzhynska's Museum in Lubny], *Kievskaya Starina* [Kyivan Antiquity], vol. 31, no. 10, pp. 123–134.

Hrepachevskyi, A 1904, 'O krashankakh i pisankakh' [About krashanky and pysanky], *Kievskaya Starina* [Kyivan Antiquity], vol. 85, no. 4, pp. 17–18.

Ilchenko, O 2015, 'Blahodiynist zhinok: Kateryna Skarzhynska – spodvyzhnytsia natsionalnoi osvity Lubenshchyny (1854–1932)' [Charity of women: Kateryna Skarzhynska, a supporter of national education in Lubny region (1854–1932)], *Pedahohichni Nauky* [Pedagogical Science], no. 64, pp. 103–109.

Ivanchenko, Y 1995, 'Vydatnyi vchenyi i patriot Ukrainy' [A remarkable Ukrainian scientist and patriot], in F Vovk, *Studii z Ukrainskoi Etnohrafii ta Antropolohii* [Studies on Ukrainian Ethnography and Anthropology], Mystetstvo, Kyiv, pp. 3–6.

Ivanov, P 1889, *Igry Krestyanskikh Detey v Kupyanskom Uezde* [Games of Peasant Children in Kupyansk County], K Shchasna, Kharkiv.

Kalinskiy, I 1877, 'Tserkovno-narodnyi mesiatseslov na Rusi' [Ecclesiastical and folk menologium in Rus], *Zapiski Imperatorskogo Russkogo Geograficheskogo Obshchestva po*

Otdeleniyu Etnografii [Notes of Ethnography Division, Russian Imperial Geographical Society], vol. 7, pp. 269–480.

Karazin, N (il.) 1885, 'Svetloe Khristovo Voskresenje v derevne' [Bright Easter Sunday in a village], *Niva*, no. 12, pp. 276–277.

Kharuzin, N 1889, 'O noydakh u drevnikh i sovremennykh loparey' [About shamans among ancient and modern Lapps], *Etnograficheskoe Obozrenie* [Ethnographic Review], book 1, pp. 36–76.

Kobrynska, N & Pchilka, O (eds.) 1887, *Pershyi Vinok* [First Wreath], Tovarystvo im. Shevchenko [The Shevchenko Society], Lviv.

Kolbe, W 1888, *Hessische Volks-Sitten und Gebräuche im Lichte der Heidnischen Vorzeit* [Hessian Folk Customs and Traditions in the Light of Pagan Antiquity], N. G. Elwert, Marburg.

Kolberg, O 1882, *Pokucie: Obraz Etnograficzny* [Pokuttia: Ethnographic Portrait], O Kolberg, Krakow.

Kondratovych, O 1883, 'Zadunaiskaya Sech za mestnymi vospominaniyami i rasskazami' [The Transdanube Sich according to the local recollections and stories], *Kievskaya Starina* [Kyivan Antiquity], vol. 1, pp. 27–67, vol. 2, pp. 269–300 & vol. 4, pp. 728–773.

Koropchevskiy, D (ed. & trans.) 1874, *Basni i Skazki Dikikh Narodov* [Fables and Folk Tales of Wild Peoples], (Translation of Bleek, W 1864, *Reynard the Fox in South Africa* and Callaway, H 1868, *Nursery Tales, Traditions and Histories of the Zulus*)], (in 2 vols.), V Demakov, Saint Petersburg.

Kosach, O 1876, *Ukrainskiy Narodnyi Ornament: Vyshyvki, Tkani, Pisanky* [Ukrainian Folk Ornament: Embroidery, Fabrics and Pysanky], S V Kulzhenko, Kyiv.

Kozar, L 2007, 'Postat Vasylia Horlenka v istoryko-kulturnomu zhytti Ukrainy' [Persona of Vasyl Horlenko within historical and cultural life of Ukraine], *Materialy do Ukrainskoi Etnolohii* [Materials on Ukrainian Ethnology], no. 6(X), pp. 210–216.

Kraskii, T 1705, *Dissertatio de Ovo Paschali* [Dissertation on Easter eggs], Lipsiae, Regiomonti, Martinum Hallervord, Frankfurt (Oder).

Kulish, P 1856–57, *Zapiski o Yuzhnoy Rusi* [Notes on Southern Rus], (in 2 vols.), P Kulish, Saint Petersburg.

Kulzhynskyi, S 1899, *Opisanie Kollektsii Narodnykh Pisanok* [Description of Folk Pysanky Collection], Lubenskiy muzey E. N. Skarzhinskoy: Etnograficheskiy Otdel [Skarzhynska Museum in Lubny: Ethnographic Department], Moscow.

Kvitka-Osnovyanenko, H 1833, 'Soldatskyi portret' [A soldier's portrait], *Almanakh Utrenniaya Zvezda* [Morning Star Almanac], book 2, pp. 9–43.

Kvitka-Osnovyanenko, H 1837, 'Ot tobi i skarb' [Here is a treasure for you], *Malorosiyskie Povesti Rasskazyvaemye Hrytskom Osnovyanenkom* [Ukrainian Novels Told by Hrytsko Osnovyanenko], book 2, Lazarevyi, Moscow.

Lauterbach, H & Jensen, J 1706, *Dissertatio de Tripudio Solis Paschali* [Dissertation on Celebration of Easter Sunday], Helmstedt, Hamm.

Lazarevskyi, O 1875, 'Ocherki malorossiyskikh familiy. Materialy dlia istorii obshchestva v 17 i 18 vekakh: Hamaley, Hertsiki, Hoholi-Yanovskie' [Sketches on Ukrainian families. Materials on 18–19th centuries society history: the Hamaley, Hertsiki and Hoholi families], *Russkiy Arkhiv* [Russian Archive], book 4, pp. 439–452.

Levchenko, M 1875, 'Neskolko dannykh o zhilishche i pishche yuzhnorusov' [Some data on houses and food of the Southern Rus natives], *Zapiski Yugo-Zapadnogo Otdela Imperatorskogo Russkogo Geograficheskogo Obshchestva* [Notes of South-Western Division, Russian Imperial Geographical Society], vol. 2, pp. 135–150.

Lozynskyi, I 1859, 'Halahyvka' [Halahyvka: Easter games], *Zoria Halytska: Yako Album na God 1860* [Galician Morning Star 1860 Almanac], Stavropyiskyi Institute, Lviv.

Lönnrot, E 1835–36, *Kalewala taikka wanhoja Karjalan runoja Suomen kansan muinosista ajoista* [The Old Kalevala], 2 vols, J C Frenckellin ja Poika, Helsinki.

Maksymovych, M 1856, 'Dni i mesiatsy ukrainskogo selianina' [The days and months of a Ukrainian villager], *Russkaya Beseda* [Russian Conversation], book 1, pp. 61–83.

Maksymovych, M 1876–80, *Sobranie Sochineniy* [Collected Works], (in 3 vols.), M P Frits, Kyiv.

Mandebura, O 2011, *Mykola Sumtsov i Problemy Sotsiokulturnoi Identychnosti* [Mykola Sumtsov and Problems of Socio-Cultural Identity], Natsionalna Akademia Nauk Ukrainy [The National Academy of Sciences of Ukraine], Kyiv.

Maspero, G 1882, *Les Contes Populaires de* l'Égypte Ancienne [Popular Tales of Ancient Egypt], J Maisonneuve, Paris.

Mazurewicz, F 1889, 'Zdobywanie jaj i pisanki w Syberji Wschodniej' [Collecting eggs and pysanky in Eastern Siberia], *Wisła*, vol. 4, book 4, pp. 713–714.

Metlynskyi, A 1854, *Narodnye Yuzhnorusskie Pesni* [The Southern Rus Folk Songs], Kyiv University Publishing, Kyiv.

Michajlyszyn, R 2015, 'Rol dekoratyvno-prykladnoho mystetstva u formuvanni mizhkulturnoi kompetentsii' [The role of applied arts in the formation of intercultural competence], *Naukowe Akademii im. Jana Długosza w Częstochowie: Rocznik Polsko-Ukraiński* [Scientific Research of the Jan Długosz University in Częstochowa: Polish-Ukrainian Yearbook], vol. 17, pp. 491–498.

Minaev, I 1876, *Indiyskie Skazki i Legendy, Sobrannye v Kamaone v 1875 Godu* [Indian Folk Tales and Legends, Gathered in Kumaon in 1875], Demakov, Saint Petersburg.

Mykhalevych, I 2019, *Ukrainska Narodna Pysanka* [Ukrainian Folk Pysanka], Klub Simeynoho Dozvillia [Family Entertainment Club], Kharkiv.

'Neskolko slov o tom, kak prigotovliayut pisanki i krashanki' [A few words on how to make pysanky and krahanky] 1903, *Kievskaya Starina* [Kyivan Antiquity], vol. 82, no. 9, pp. 105–106.

Nomys, M (ed.) 1864, *Ukrainski Pryslivya, Prykazky i Take Inshe* [Ukrainian Proverbs, Sayings and the Like], V Drukarniakh Tyblen i Komp. I Kulish [In Printing House of Tyblen and Kulish], Saint Petersburg.

Nomys, M 1898, 'Krashanky v starinu' [Krashanky in the old days], *Kievskaya Starina* [Kyivan Antiquity], vol. 61, no. 4, pp. 9–10.

Nowosielski, A 1857, *Lud Ukrainski, jego Piesni, Bajki, Podania, Klechdy, Zabobony, Obrzedy, Zwyczaje, Przyslowia, Zagadki, Zamawiania,*

Sekreta Lekarskie, Ubiory, Tance, Gry i t. d. [Ukrainian People, their Songs, Legends, Administration, Tales, Superstitions, Rituals, Customs, Proverbs, Riddles, etc.], (in 2 vols.), Glücksberg, Wilno.

Odarchenko, P 1985, 'Skarbnytsia ukrainskoho slova' [A treasury of Ukrainian word], *Collection of Folklore by Matviy Nomys: in Commemoration of the 120th Anniversary of the First Edition 1864–1984*, The Publishing Fund of His Beatitude Metropolitan Mstyslav, Primate of the Ukrainian Autocephalous Orthodox Church in the Diaspora, South Bound Brook, N J, pp. 9–24.

Pavlutskyi, H 1889, *Drevnegrecheskie Raspisnye Vazy* [Ancient Greek Ornamented Vases], Tovarishchestvo Pechatnogo Dela [Printing Business Association], Kyiv.

Paziak, M 1993, 'M Nomys i zbirka Ukrainski Prykazky, Pryslivya i Take Inshe' [M Nomys and his collection of Ukrainian Proverbs, Sayings and the Like], in M Nomys, *Ukrainski Prykazky, Pryslivya i Take Inshe* [Ukrainian Proverbs, Sayings and the Like] Lybid, Kyiv, pp. 5–25.

Pchilka, O 1903, 'Ukrainskie koliadki' [Ukrainian koliadky], *Kievskaya Starina* [Kyivan Antiquity], vol. 1, pp. 152–175, vol. 4, pp. 132–160, vol. 5, pp. 192–230 & vol. 6, pp. 347–394.

Pchilka, O 1925, 'Ukrainski narodni lehendy ostannioho chasu' [Ukrainian folk legends of the modern times], *Etnohrafichnyi Visnyk* [Ethnographic Herald], book 1, pp. 41–49.

Pchilka, O 1929, 'Ukrainian selianske maliuvannia na stinakh' [Ukrainian village painting on walls], *Zapysky Istorychno-Filolohichnoho Viddilu Akademii Nauk* [Notes of the Historical and Philological Department of the Ukrainian Academy of Sciences], book 23, pp. 177–188.

Petrow, A 1878, 'Lud ziemi Dobrzyńskiej, jego charakter, mowa, zwyczaje, obrzedy, pieśni, przysłowia, zagadki itp.' [People of Dobrzyń region, their character, speech, customs, rites, songs, proverbs, riddles, etc.], *Zbiór Wiadomości do Antropologii Krajowej* [Collection of Reports on the National Anthropology], vol. 2, pp. 3–182.

Potebnia, O 1883–87, *Obyasneniya Malorusskikh i Srodnykh Pesen (Koliadky i Shchedrivky)* [Commentaries on Ukrainian and akin Songs (Koliadky and Shchedrivky)], (in 2 vols.), M Zamkevych, Warsaw.

Reville, A 1883, *Histoire des Religions: Les Religions des Peuples Non-Civilisés* [History of Religions: Religions of Uncivilised Peoples], (in 2 vols.), Fischbacher, Paris.

Richier, A 1682, 'Dissertatio de Ovis Paschalibus – von Ostereiern' [Dissertation on Easter Eggs], in Georg Franck von Franckenau, *Satyrae Medicae*, Heidelberg University, Heidelberg.

Romanov, E 1887, *Belorusskiy Sbornik. Vypusk Tretiy: Skazki* [Belarusian Anthology. Third Issue: Folk Tales], G. A. Malkin, Vitebsk.

Roslavskyi-Petrovskyi, O 1865–69, *Rukovodstvo k Istorii Glavnykh Narodov Drevnego Vostoka i Ikh Tsivilizatsii: Egipet i Khaldeya* [Guide to History of the Major Peoples of the Ancient East and Their Civilizations: Egypt and Chaldea], (in 2 vols.), Kharkiv University Publishing, Kharkiv.

Rudynska, E 1927, 'V. P. Horlenko', *Zapysky Istorychno-Filolohichnoho Viddilu VUAN* [Notes of the Historical and Philological Department, the National Academy of Sciences of Ukraine], book 12, pp. 304–318.

Rybalko, P 2010, *Kolektsiya Pysanok Volodymyra Yastrebova* [Volodymyr Yastrebov's Pysanky Collection], Kirovohrad Local History Museum, Kirovohrad.

Sadovnikov, D 1884, 'Skazki i Predaniya Samarskogo Kraya' [Folk Tales and Legends of Samara Region], *Zapiski Imperatorskogo Russkogo Geograficheskogo Obshchestva po Otdeleniyu Etnografii* [Notes of Ethnography Division, Russian Imperial Geographical Society], vol. 12.

Sadowska, J 1890, 'Pisanki' [Pysanky], *Wisła*, vol. 4, book 2, pp. 461–462.

Saltykov-Shchedrin, M 1889–90, 'Poshekhonskaya starina' [Old years in Poshekhonye], *Sobranie Sochineniy* [Collected Works], (in 9 vols.), Author's Publishing, Saint Petersburg.

'Sbornik uzorov pisanok' [A collection of pysanka patterns] 1897, *Kievskaya Starina* [Kyivan Antiquity] vol. 59, no. 11, pp. 39–41.

Sementovskyi, K 1843, 'Zamechaniya o prazdnikakh u malorosiyan' [Observations on the Ukrainians' feast days], *Mayak* [Lighthouse], vol. 11, ch. 3, pp. 1–45.

Sepp, J 1853, *Das Heidenthum und dessen Bedeutung für das Christenthum* [Paganism and its Importance for Christianity], (in 3 vols.), Regensburg, Manz.

Serhienko, D 2015, 'Metsenatske podvyzhnytstvo Kateryny Skarzhynskoi' [Philantropic pursuit of Kateryna Skarzhynska], *Naukovi Pratsi Istorychnoho Fakultetu Zaporizskoho Natsionalnoho Universytetu* [Scholarly works of the Department of History, Zaporizhian National University], no. 43, pp. 151–154.

Shein, P 1874, *Belorusskie Narodnye Pesni* [Belarusian Folk Songs], Maikov, Saint Petersburg.

Stranecka, F 1888, 'O symbolice moravskych kraslicic' [About symbolism of Moravian Easter eggs], in Havelkova et al., *Moravské Ornamenty* [Moravian Ornaments], Vlastenecký Muzejní Spolek, Olomouc, pp.6–11.

Struk, H (ed.) 1993, 'Nomys, Matvii', *Encyclopedia of Ukraine*, (in 5 vols.), University of Toronto Press, Toronto, vol. 3, p. 609.

Sumtsov, M 1881, *O Svadebnykh Obriadakh* [On Wedding Traditions], I V Popov, Kharkiv.

Sumtsov, M 1885, *Religiozno-Mificheskoe Znachenie Malorusskoi Svadby* [Religious and Mythical Meaning of Ukrainian Wedding], Izdanie Redaktsii 'Kievskoy Stariny' [Kyivan Antiquity Editorial Board Publishing], Kyiv.

Sumtsov, M 1886, 'Nauchnoe izuchenie koliadok i shchedrivok' [Scientific studies on koliadky i shchedrivky], *Kievskaya Starina* [Kyivan Antiquity], vol. 14, no. 2, pp. 237–266.

Sumtsov, M 1889, 'Obriadovoe yaytso' [Ritual egg], *Kievskaya Starina* [Kyivan Antiquity], vol. 26, no. 7, pp. 35–37.

Sumtsov, M 1891, 'Pysanky', *Kievskaya Starina* [Kyivan Antiquity], vol. 33, no. 5, pp. 181–209 & vol. 33, no. 6, pp. 363–383.

Sumtsov, M 1893, 'Lehenda o hreshnoy materi' [A legend about a sinful mother], *Kievskaya Starina* [Kyivan Antiquity], vol. 41, no. 5, pp. 195–207.

Sumtsov, M 1895, 'O vliyanii malorusskoi skholasticheskoy literatury XVII v. na velykorusskuyu raskolnicheskuyu literaturu XVIII v. i ob otrazhenii v raskolnicheskoi literature massonstva.' [On influence of the Ukrainian scholastic literature of the 17th century on the Russian schismatic literature of the 18th century and on manifestation of masonry in the schismatic literature], *Kievskaya Starina* [Kyivan Antiquity], vol. 51, no. 12, pp. 367–378.

Sumtsov, M 1906, *O Literaturnykh Nravakh Yuzhnorusskikh Pisateley XVII st.* [On Literary Tendencies of the Ukrainian Writers of the 17th century], Tipografiya Imperatorskoy Akademii Nauk [Printing House of the Imperial Academy of Sciences], Saint Petersburg.

Svitlic, D 1889, 'Uskršnja šarena jaja' [Colorful Easter eggs], *Glasnik Zemaljskog Muzeja Bosne i Hercegovine* [Herald of the National Museum of Bosnia and Herzegovina], year 1, book 3, pp. 60–62.

Tereshchenko, A 1848, *Byt Russkogo Naroda* [Daily Life of the Russian People], (in 7 vols.), Ministerstvo Vnutrennikh Del [Ministry of Internal Affairs], Saint Petersburg.

Trachevskyi, A 1884, 'Popytka primeneniya evoliutsionnoy teorii k arkheologii' [An attempt to apply the evolutionary theory to archaeology], *Trudy Shestogo Arkheologicheskogo Sjezda (v Odesse)* [Works of the Sixth Archaeological Congress (in Odesa)], vol. 4, pp. 1–25.

Tylor, E 1881, *Anthropology: an Introduction to the Study of Man and Civilization*, Macmillan and Co, London.

Tytarenko, V 2009, 'Naukovets-etnohraf kintsia XIX pochatku XX stolittia Olena Pchilka' [Olena Pchilka, a scientist-ethnographer of the late 19th and early 20th centuries], *Vytoky Pedahohichnoi Maisternosti. Seriya: Pedahohichni Nauky* [Origins of Pedagogical Mastery. Series: Pedagogical Sciences], no. 6, pp. 110–113.

Udziela, S 1888, *Piski w Mieście Ropczycach i Okolicy* [Pysanky in Ropczyce and Surrounding Area], Pogoni, Tarnow.

Ulanowska, S 1884, 'Niektore materialy etnograficzne we wsi Ludowe (mazowieckim) zebrane' [Some ethnographic materials collected in Mazovia province villages], *Zbiór Wiadomości do Antropologii Krajowej* [Collection of Reports on the National Anthropology], vol. 8, pp. 247–323.

Uspenskiy, H 1818, *Opyt Povestvovania o Drevnostiakh Russkikh* [Essay on Tales about Rus' Antiquity], V Universitetskoy Tipografii [University Publishing], Kharkiv.

Vasnetsov, V (il.) 1885, 'Khristos voskres!' [Christ is risen!], *Niva*, no. 12, p. 289.

Voevodskyi, L 1874, *Kannibalism v Hrecheskikh Mifakh. Opyt Istorii Razvitiya Nravstvennosti* [Cannibalism in Greek Myths: Essay on the History of Development of Morality], V. S. Balashev, Saint Petersburg.

Volkov, F 1878, 'Otlichitelnye cherty yuzhnorusskoy narodnoy ornamentiki' [Characteristic features of the Southern Rus folk ornamentation], *Trudy Tretiego Arkheologicheskogo Sjezda (v Kieve)* [Works of the Third Archaeological Congress (in Kyiv)], vol. 2, pp. 317–326.

Volters, E 1890, *Materialy dlia Etnohrafii Latyshskogo Plemeni Vitebskoy Hubernii* [Ethnography Materials on the Latvian People in Vitebsk Province], Tipografiya Imperatorskoi Akademii Nauk [Imperial Academy of Sciences Publishing], Saint Petersburg.

Vyshnevska, N 1988, 'Olena Pchilka', in O Pchilka, *Tvory* [Works], Dnipro, Kyiv, pp. 5–26.

Wankel, J 1888, 'Ornamenty na kraslicich moravskych' [Ornaments on Moravian Easter eggs] in Havelkova et al., *Moravské Ornamenty* [Moravian Ornaments], Vlastenecký Muzejní Spolek, Olomouc, pp. 12–31.

Wanklova, M (il.) 1888, in Havelkova et al., *Moravské Ornamenty* [Moravian Ornaments], Vlastenecký Muzejní Spolek, Olomouc.

Wolski, Z & Dowgird, T 1890, 'Pisanki, jajka malowane wielkanocne: Poszukiwanie' [Research: pysanky, painted eggs for Easter], *Wisła*, vol. 4, supplement.

Wunderlich, G 1884, *Das Christliche Kirchenjahr* [Christian Church Year], F.W.L. Dreßler, Bad Langensalza.

Yastrebov, V 1886, *Obychai i Pesni Turetskikh Serbov* [Customs and Songs of the Turkish Serbs], V. S. Balashev, Saint Petersburg.

Yastrebov, V 1893, *Malorusskie Prozvishcha Khersonskoi Hubernii* [Ukrainian Surnames in Kherson Province], Tip. V. V. Kirkhner [The Printing House of V. V. Kirkhner], Odesa.

Yastrebov, V 1894, *Materialy po Etnografii Novorossiyskogo Kraya, Sobrannye v Elisavegradskom i Aleksandriyskom Uezdakh Khersonskoy Hubernii* [Materials on the Ethnography of Novorossiysk Region, Collected in Elysavethrad and Oleksandria Counties of Kherson Province], Tip. Sht. Odesskogo Voennogo Okruga [The Printing House of Odesa Military District Headquarters], Odesa.

Yastrebov, V 1895, 'Neskolko slov o pisankakh' [A few words on Pysanky], *Kievskaya Starina* [Kyivan Antiquity], vol. 49, no. 4, pp. 5–8.

Yastrebov, V 1897, 'Svadebnye obriadnye khleby v Malorosii' [Ritual wedding breads in Ukraine], *Kievskaya Starina* [Kyivan Antiquity], vol. 59, no. 11, pp. 281–288.

Zabelin, I 1862, *Domashniy Byt Russkikh Tsarey v XVI i XVII Stoletiyakh* [Everyday Life of Russian Tsars in the 16th and 17th Centuries], V. Grachev and Co., Moscow.

Zibrt, C 1889, *Staroceske Vyrocni Obyceje, Povery, Slavnosti a Zabavy Prostonarodni* [Ancient Czech Yearly Folk Customs, Superstitions, Celebrations and Entertainment], JR Vilimka, Prague.

Zibrt, C 1890, 'Nektere wyklady of puvoda kraslic' [Some interpretations on the origin of Easter eggs], *Zpráva Společnosti Přátel Starožitností Českých v Praze* [Report of the Czech Society of Friends of Antiquities in Prague], no. 2, p. 33.

Zmigrodzki, M 1889, 'Miedzynarodowy Kongres: Folklorystow w Paryzu roku 1889' [International Congress of Folklorists in Paris, 1889], *Wisła*, vol. 4, book 4, pp. 969–982.

Glossary

Fern Flower – In Ukrainian folklore, it is almost impossible to find *fern flower*, which blossoms only once a year for a very brief period of time and is guarded by evil forces. However, the lucky ones who find the *fern flower* will acquire magic powers to understand animals, to find hidden treasures and others.

Firebird (Ukr., *zhar-ptytsia* or *zhar-ptakh*) – In Slavic folklore this bird with golden and dazzling fire-like feathers lives in a faraway land or the kingdom of Sun. It brings good fortune and love.

Galician Rus (alternatively, *Halytska Rus*) – This archaic term along with its synonym *Red Rus* (Ukr., *Chervona Rus*) appeared in academic publications in the first half of the 19th century and was referred to Galicia (*Halychyna*), a region in Western Ukraine.

Green Week – Also known as *Klechalnyi* or *Rusalnyi* (derived from *rusalka*), *Green Week* ('Zelenyi Tyzhden' in Ukrainian) falls before Pentecost. The name 'klechalnyi' is derived from 'klechannia', meaning 'green plants' or 'greenery'. During this week, among other rituals, the villagers decorate their houses with green twigs and wild flowers and herbs; one function of this is to protect the house from evil forces.

Hrobky Week – Also known as *Provody, Radovnytsia, Radunytsia, Didy, Pomynalna nedilia, Mavka* and so on, *Hrobky Week* follows Easter Week, that is, the second week after Easter, and is traditionally dedicated to commemorating the departed friends and relatives. The ceremonies include church memorial services and visiting the graves.

Hryvni (plural; *hryvnia*, singular) – Ukrainian *hryvnia* is the official currency of Ukraine. In practice, the *hryvnia* is divided into 100 smaller *kopiyka* units.

Ivan Tsarevych – Also known as, *Ivan, the Tsar's son*, in Slavic folklore, *Ivan Tsarevych* is a protagonist hero of some folk tales.

Khrestopoklonna Nedilia – On the third Sunday of the Great Lent a special church service is held, where the Holy Cross is honoured with particular reverence. *Khrestopoklonna Nedilia* literally means 'Bowing-to-the-Cross Sunday'.

Khrystosuvannia – see the definition of *khrystosuvatysia*.

Khrystosuvatysia – The Ukrainian ritual to *khrystosuvatysia* takes place in the time of Easter celebrations and consists of exchanging Easter greetings. During this period, when relatives, friends or acquaintances meet, they greet each other: 'Christ is risen!', to which the reply is: 'Truly, He is risen!'. Then they kiss each other on the cheek three times. Often this 'triple-kissing', in particular, is called *khrystosuvatysia*. During this ritual it also was customary to exchange *pysanky* or *krashanky*. In his article *Pysanky*, Mykola Sumtsov, also mentions *khrystosuvatysia* in relation to two other rituals that used to take place in some parts of Ukraine. In one instance, *khrystosuvatysia* refers to a beekeeper greeting his bees with *pysanka*. It was believed that having performed this ritual would result in bees multiplying hundredfold and be healthy. In the other instance the word *khrystosuvatysia* was used to call the ritual games, during which the villagers 'greeted' *rusalky*. *Khrystosuvannia* is a noun derived from *khrystosuvatysia*.

Kniaz (singular; *Kniazi*, plural) – *Kniaz* (Velykyi [Engl., 'Great]) was the title of the supreme male ruler of Kyiv (*Kniahynia*, female) and its principalities during the 9th to 13th centuries in Kyivan Rus. The translations of this title into the English language, although not very precise, include Grand Prince, or Grand Duke.

Kniazhna (singular; *Kniazhny*, plural) – Also known as *Kniazivna*, *Kniazhna* was the title of an unmarried daughter of a *Kniaz* (see definition).

Koliadky (plural; *koliadka*, singular) – Also known as *koliadkas* or *kolyadky*, these ritual songs survived since pre-Christian times when they were performed during winter solstice celebrations.

With introduction of the Christianity the ritual songs were adopted into Christmas celebrations and in Ukraine are usually performed on 7 January. *Koliadky* or analogous songs are known to other Slavic nations.

Kopiyky (plural; *kopiyka,* singular) – Is a monetary unit in Ukraine that equals 1/100 of the *hryvnia.*

Korovai (singular; *korovaii,* plural) – Also known as *korovay,* this ritual bread is round in form and ornately ornamented with baked-on dough birds, flowers, grapes and so on. It is an essential part of the wedding rituals in Ukraine as well as some other events celebrated according to folk customs.

Kosh Bessmertnyi (Russ., also known as, *Koshchey Bessmertnyi;* Ukr., *Kostiy Bezdushnyi* or *Koshchiy Bezsmertnyi* [Deathless]) – In Slavic folklore, *Kosh Bessmertnyi* is an antagonist character of some folk tales.

Krashanka (singular; *krashanky,* plural) – Along with the *pysanka,* the *krashanka* is the most popular of the Ukrainian traditional Easter eggs. *Krashanky* are usually one-colour dyed eggs and they are edible: the raw eggs are boiled in a dyeing solution.

Paska (singular; *pasky,* plural) – In Ukrainian culture, this ritual Easter bread is one of the main symbols of Easter.

Pysanka (singular; *pysanky,* plural) – This exquisitely ornate Ukrainian Easter egg was customarily given as a gift on the occasion of Easter. In addition to passing good wishes to its recipient, *pysanka* has many other meanings and roles in Ukrainian culture. Recipients of *pysanka* keep it as talisman. Folklore offers intriguing tales and legends featuring *pysanka.* Academics research its origins, diversity and features. As a subject of applied folk art, it is praised for its elegance and originality.

Rakhman – see *Rakhmanskyi Velykden.*

Rakhmanskyi Velykden – Also known as *Prava Sereda* or *Sukha Sereda,* this a folk holiday falls on Feast of Mid-Pentecost, which is celebrated on the 25th day after Easter (Ukr., *Velykden*). *Rakhmanskyi* is an adjective derived from *Rakhman* (*Rakhmany,* plural). According to some Ukrainian folk beliefs, *Rakhmany* were their ancestors, the most righteous men, who lived in a mythical faraway land. Other beliefs considered *Rakhmany* to be Christians, who lived in India. On the day of *Rakhmanskyi Velykden* (or *'Rakhmany's Easter'*), there was a ritual in some areas of Ukraine, to place *krashanky* eggshells in rivers, believing that the current will carry the eggshells to *Rakhmany*. On receiving the eggshells they would know that Easter has arrived.

Rozhovyny – Consumption of the first non-Lenten meal after Lent has a special term in Ukrainian *rozhovyny*. *Rozhovyny*, which takes place the day following Great Lent, in other words on Easter, is filled with many rituals; one of them is that the first food that is consumed should be the one that was blessed at church, for example, *krashanky*. *Rozhivliatysia* is the verb referring to the act of *rozhovyny*.

Rusalky (plural; *rusalka*, singular) – A mythological female figure, the *rusalka* is a kind of nymph. *Rusalky* share some similar characteristics with mermaids but have a very distinct nature that was developed through centuries of Ukrainian mythology. In Ukrainian mythology, the *rusalky* are the souls of young women, often brides, who have died an unnatural death, such as drowning or suicide. They prefer to live in standing water – ponds or rivers that are still or have a slow-moving current. Usually, they come out from water in the warm months during the new moon. *Rusalky* are beautiful young women. They are dressed in long, white thin shirts or are naked. *Rusalky* entice young men, luring them with their songs. They tickle them to death and take their bodies under the water. They also kill women if after giving them a riddle the latter does not give the correct answer.

Shchedrivky (plural; *shchedrivka*, singular) – Also known as *shchedrivkas*, these ritual songs are related to *koliadky*, since among other things, they are performed annually during winter celebrations. The main differences between the two are that *koliadky* are performed on the occasion of Christmas, praise the birth of Jesus and are usually performed on 7 January; whereas *shchedrivky* are sung on the occasion of the New Year, praise and convey good wishes to the persons they are sung for and usually performed on 14 January.

Southern Rus – (also, South-Western Rus) a term often used by 19th scholars in their works referring to some regions of Ukraine, including Kyiv, Volyn, Chernihiv and others.

Tomyna Sunday – Also known as *Tomyna Nedilia, Fomyna Sunday, Anti-Easter* (in the sense of 'instead of Easter') *Khomyna Sunday, Providna Sunday* and so on, is Sunday that follows Easter Sunday and falls on *Hrobky Week*. 'Tomyna', 'Fomyna' and 'Khomyna' are possessive nouns and mean 'Toma's', 'Foma's' and 'Khoma's', all of which are Ukrainian versions of the name of Thomas the Apostle. The day received its name after the event described in the Bible, when resurrected Jesus appeared to Thomas the Apostle.

Upyri (plural; *upyr,* singular) – These mythological 'undead' beings, most often male, are said to rise from the grave at night and attack people and animals in order to suck their blood. *Upyri* are the predecessors of Western vampires and share some similar characteristics with them. *Upyri* were once living people who suffered a sudden unnatural death, such as drowning or freezing to death, or those who committed suicide, or were cursed (damned) by their relatives. *Upyri* are friendly with witches and help them in their evil sorcery.

Editorial Note

This book is a part of *Ukrainian Scholar Library* series, a collection of academic writings on a broad range of topics produced by Ukrainian scholars throughout the centuries.

The present publication contains works of a number of authors, both experts and amateurs in the field of ethnology. In his foreword Pavlo Rybalko provides brief information on some of the authors as well as other notable personas mentioned in the book.

The articles in the publication do not adhere to strict chronological order. The first article, Mykola Sumtsov's 'Pysanky' (1891), is placed first, since it is the most comprehensive work on the subject in the collection.

This is the first English translation of the articles. The present translation uses the words 'Ukraine' and 'Ukrainians' in place of 'Malorosiya' [Little Russia] and 'Malorosy' [Little Russians], which were used in the original texts.

On the basis that the words 'Ukraine' ('Ukrainian') and Easter are used in the texts very frequently, they are not included in the indexes as separate entries.

The Ukrainian names of ornaments, personal names and some geographical names are transliterated to reflect their spelling in the original language.

The footnotes and comments in square brackets throughout the text are made by the translator, unless otherwise indicated.

Mykola Sumtsov's article 'Pysanky' (1891) is amended in this edition to include chapter titles throughout the text as opposed to their original position, at the beginning of the article in a way of a table of contents.

Some parts of the texts have been heavily edited. Where possible in-text references and Bibliography entries were amended, as for example, to include the author's name and page numbers.

Since the book is printed in black and white some of the illustrations have been digitally amended to enhance visibility of necessary details.

The illustration on the cover depicts 'Berehynia' symbol, which was used as an emblem of 2015 All-Ukrainian Pysanky Festival.

Index of
Geographical Names

Index of
Religious, Philosophical and Mythological Names

See also 'Index of personalities' on page 166.

Index of
Pysanka Symbols

Index of
Personalities

See also 'Index of religious, philosophical and mythological names' on page 161.

Sova Books'
Ukrainian Scholar Library

Coming Soon

Collection of Ukrainian Spells
Petro Yefymenko

The Cure Beneath Our Feet
Yuriy Lypa

Ukrainian Folk Worldview: A Sketch of Ukrainian Mythology
Ivan Nechui-Levytskyi

Notes on Ukrainian Demonology
Vasyl Myloradovych

Skovoroda's Morals
Eugen Hlywa (ed.)

www.ingramcontent.com/pod-product-compliance
Lightning Source LLC
Chambersburg PA
CBHW060512290526
45791CB00001B/365